David Campbell

Wood in Traditional Architecture

Schiffer Publishing Ltd

Other Schiffer Books By The Author:
Stone in Traditional Architecture. ISBN: 9780764336140. $45.00

Other Schiffer Books on Related Subjects:
Colonial Architecture: Early Examples from the First State. George Fletcher Bennett Foreword by Bernie Herman. ISBN: 0764325108. $29.95
Early Domestic Architecture of Pennsylvania. Eleanor Raymond, Introduction by R. Brognard Okie. ISBN: 0764325906. $29.95
German Architecture in America. Irwin Richman. ISBN: 0764318004. $49.95
Half-Timber Architecture. Tina Skinner. ISBN: 9780764326677. $39.95
Shaker Architecture. Herbert Schiffer. ISBN: 0887401538. $24.95
Spanish Revival Architecture. Jerry "S. F." Cook III, Tina Skinner. ISBN: 0764323091. $49.95

Library of Congress Control Number: 2010937373

Cover designed by: Bruce Waters
Type set in DeVinne BT/Zurich BT

ISBN: 978-0-7643-3581-5
Printed in China

Schiffer Books are available at special discounts for bulk purchases for sales promotions or premiums. Special editions, including personalized covers, corporate imprints, and excerpts can be created in large quantities for special needs. For more information contact the publisher:

Published by Schiffer Publishing Ltd.
4880 Lower Valley Road
Atglen, PA 19310
Phone: (610) 593-1777; Fax: (610) 593-2002
E-mail: Info@schifferbooks.com

For the largest selection of fine reference books on this and related subjects, please visit our web site at
www.schifferbooks.com
We are always looking for people to write books on new and related subjects. If you have an idea for a book please contact us at the above address.

This book may be purchased from the publisher.
Include $5.00 for shipping.
Please try your bookstore first.
You may write for a free catalog.

In Europe, Schiffer books are distributed by
Bushwood Books
6 Marksbury Ave.
Kew Gardens
Surrey TW9 4JF England
Phone: 44 (0) 20 8392 8585; Fax: 44 (0) 20 8392 9876
E-mail: info@bushwoodbooks.co.uk
Website: www.bushwoodbooks.co.uk

Contents

Introduction

This book is the first of a series of three exploring the use of natural materials – wood, earth, and stone – in traditional architecture. By "traditional", we mean that which is culturally transmitted from generation to generation within a society over a lengthy period of time. Our building traditions, and those of most folk arts, evolved only slowly over the centuries, up until the beginnings of the industrial era, which suddenly and radically changed habits and practices, and broke with tradition.

We have chosen to center this study of wood on Europe, continent with which the author feels the most affinity, as the entire world is too vast to consider in just one book. Even having concentrated on this small but culturally rich part of the world, we felt obliged to limit the study to only the most important of regional differences, a vast subject in itself. For each country is made up of many different regions, each with its own resources and with hundreds of years of more or less separate and independent development. And each region in its turn is subdivided into territories, each having its own personality and characteristics, which ethnologists, and those architects interested in local traditions, can talk to you about at length.

As we have not tried to summarize the world in this volume, neither is it our intention to give a summary of the architecture of each country, but rather, to help the reader to understand the systems of construction which make up this architectural heritage. These go beyond national and even cultural boundaries; thus we have often presented, on a same double page, examples from two or more countries to illustrate a common principle.

We hope that you will enjoy these pictures, and that they will contribute to a greater appreciation of our European building heritage. These traditions, already over a thousand years old, were brought to the New World during the period of French and of English colonization, and were reinforced throughout the nineteenth century by the different waves of immigration from Eastern Europe, Central Europe, and Scandinavia. They were thus of fundamental importance in the settlement of North America.

Apart from their esthetic side, we also admire that many of these constructions – excluding the churches and the town houses – were built by farmers or settlers having no specialized training in building crafts, working only with simple tool and techniques. One of the author's goals is to bring these back to mind – for they are part, for many of you, of your ancestral memory – and to remind you that if you have time and energy available, you can build your own home, as did a large part of the population in centuries past.

Whether your goal be to reappropriate your autonomy or simply to know more about the past and about our architectural heritage, we hope you will find means and inspiration in these pages.

David Campbell
Aix-en-Provence
May 21, 2007

www.architrad-books.com

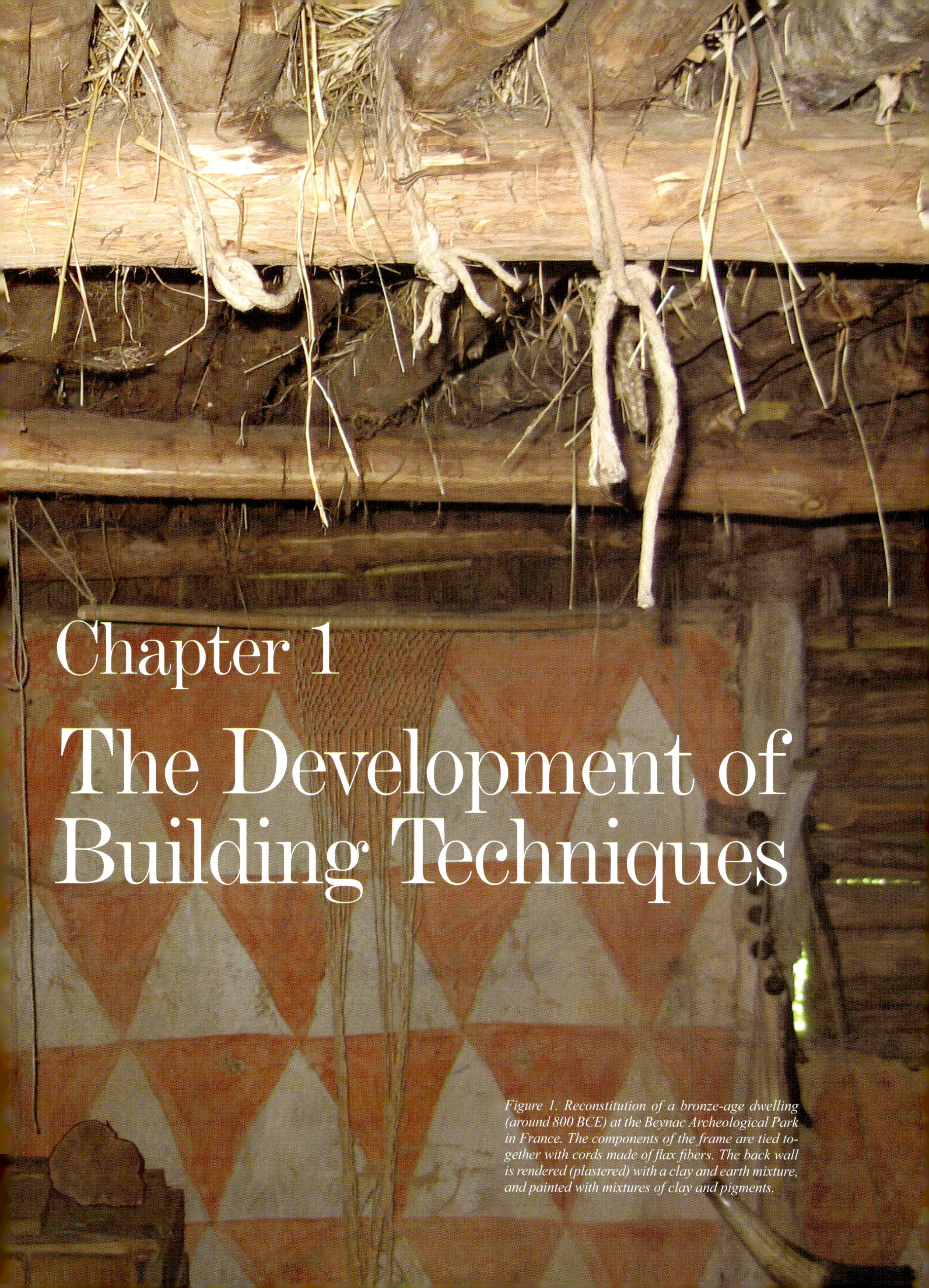

Chapter 1

The Development of Building Techniques

Figure 1. Reconstitution of a bronze-age dwelling (around 800 BCE) at the Beynac Archeological Park in France. The components of the frame are tied together with cords made of flax fibers. The back wall is rendered (plastered) with a clay and earth mixture, and painted with mixtures of clay and pigments.

*Figure 2. Hut from the Bronze Age (hypothetical reconstitution at the Beynac Archeological Park, France). Around the outside can be seen a fence made of branches interwoven between posts fixed into the ground (**wattle**). A similar structure is used for the walls and serves as a support for the application of the earth infill (**daub**), hence the name "wattle and daub" for this type of wall.*
*The roof of the hut in the foreground is covered with thatch; that of the larger building in the background with **shakes**, or **shingles**.*

Although we don't know how primitive humans learned to build, we can reasonably imagine that instinct led them to take shelter under the leafy canopy of a tree (when a cave was not available); from such a beginning, we can also then imagine that they would be inspired to enclose space inside of several trees growing only a few meters apart, and cover the space with leafy branches piled densely. They needed only their hands to break off the smaller branches and interweave them to make satisfactory walls: the roofs would require more attention and ingenuity, but no other tools.

The inhabitants of such shelters would soon discover that the leaves would dry out, though, and cease to be impermeable; at this point they would probably cover the interwoven branches with mud (preferably containing some clay for cohesion), and find a more efficient covering material for the roof: perhaps animal skins; perhaps reeds from the marshes tied in bundles; or palm or banana fronds, in tropical climates; or pieces of tree bark (especially birch, resistant to rot) overlapped and weighted down with clumps of earth containing grasses and their roots, which would gradually interweave and grow to form a "living roof."

With the development of cutting tools made from flakes of silex stone, it became possible to cut down trees in order to place the trunks where one wished; and so the "house" was born. In prehistoric times, though, when human beings lived by hunting and gathering, it would be better to speak of "shelters," as they were only intended to last during a season as the hunters followed the game.

With the development of societies based on agriculture, though (in Europe, about 6000 B.C.), humanity became sedentary, as people wished to stay close to their crops to nurture and to harvest them. This point in history really marks the "birth" of the house, as its occupants became motivated to spend time constructing it more solidly, being ready to stay for a few years.

Figure 3. For summer.

Figure 4. For winter.

Figures 3-4. Prehistoric Shelters. From a reconstitution of a prehistoric hunters' camp; Lejre Archeological Research Center, Denmark.

Figure 5. Beynac Archeological Park, France

Figure 6. Beynac Archeological Park, France

Figure 7. Beynac Archeological Park, France

Agriculture also led to the production of another material very useful in construction: straw – the stalks of cultivated grains of all sorts. The stalks were gathered into bundles, which were then tied to the roofing structure in layers, each layer overlapping the preceding one by a bit more than half. This technique is similar to that used earlier with wild-growing reeds in many pre-agricultural societies. Such roofs will last for five to fifty years, depending upon the species of grain (rye lasting longer than wheat, for instance), the climate, and the thought given to disposing the material in such a way that it can dry out after rainy periods and not rot. Straw can also be added to the earth mixture used for covering the walls: it adds cohesion to the mortar and limits the cracking of the clay as it dries. Walls filled with such mortar ("daub") applied to a support of interwoven branches ("wattle") provide good thermal insulation. Many sites in Europe dating from before the beginnings of metallurgy (the "bronze age" in Europe starting around 3000 years B.C.) have left us vestiges of such constructions, such as the sites of Chalain and Clairvaux in the Jura, and that of Lake Paladru, Isere, in France.

From this foundation, experience and observation led progressively to numerous improvements. Seeing that the posts rotted in the humid ground, builders adopted the technique of hardening the ends to be imbedded by charring them in fires. (Much later, they would be set on rocks). Those types of trees best suited to each specific use would have been repertoried in each region and this knowledge integrated into the traditions of its inhabitants. Likewise, places where there were clay deposits would have been noted, as well as the qualities of each and the optimum proportions with which each clay could be mixed with other elements to make daub, finish coats of rendering, or paint.

Figure 8. Lejre Archeological Research Center, Denmark

Figure 9. Beynac Archeological Park

Figure 10. Beynac Archeological Park

The most common way of fixing two pieces of wood together was to tie them with supple vines or plant stems or some kind of vegetal fiber which could be wound into ropes. But better joinery techniques were also devised; natural forks in tree trunks were used to support beams, and remains of Neolithic dwellings also show evidence that grooves or holes were sometimes cut into one piece, into which could be inserted the ends of other pieces, which were cut to fit. With the coming of the Age of Bronze (second millennium BCE) and that of iron (first millennium BCE), better-honed and more durable cutting tools became common, permitting craftsmen to improve their technical skills and their efficiency.

The technical procedures known in the neolithic period also included the splitting of logs in half, or even further splitting them into thick boards. Hardwood wedges would be inserted into a natural crack in the end of the log, and worked along its length by hammer blows until the log was split along its entire length. The same technique could be used (more easily) with shorter lengths. This created "shakes," or "shingles," thin rectangular pieces of wood that could be attached to the roof structure. Overlapping shakes sufficiently allowed them to shed rainwater. Buildings like those shown on these pages—hypothetical reconstitutions from the Beynac Archaeological Park in France or the Lejre Early History Centre in Denmark, using tools and techniques which researchers know existed at the time of the Bronze Age—were thus a common feature of the European landscape already one thousand years BCE.

Figure 11. Lejre Archeological Research Center, Denmark

Chapter 2

Frame (or "Post and Beam") Construction

Figure 12

Figures 12 and 13. Building with a framework of posts and beams, a method steaming directly from the innovations of Neolithic times, varies in complexity and finesse from very simple rural outbuildings (Figure 12: hen-house at the manor of St. Martin de la Lieue, Normandy, France), to the complex and finely worked urban houses of the Renaissance or the manor houses of the aristocracy (Figure 13: Rouen, Normandy, France).

Areas of Development of Different Construction Types

As was outlined in the preceding chapter, by 1000 BCE there already existed in central and western Europe a tradition of frame construction. This consists of a system of upright posts upon which are placed other horizontal pieces, which in turn support a roof structure covered with thatch or with wooden shingles. The spaces between the wooden posts are filled with whatever material is readily available – thatch, wattle, and daub, small logs, or stones assembled with a mud mortar. This tradition would be perpetuated in those regions where the forests continued to supply sufficient wood, which was not the case everywhere. In Greece and in the Italian peninsula, which the Romans were beginning to dominate by the middle of the first millennium B.C., these civilizations and their way of life rapidly used up the forest resources. Excessive cutting (for merchant ships, warships, siege engines, scaffolding for monumental buildings, and fuel for lime and for pottery kilns, among other things), as well as excessive animal grazing in regions of denser population than in the north, combined with a more arid climate to make forestry regeneration more difficult, and led to the quasi-depletion of forests resources around the Mediterranean by the time of Christ. The favored building material of these regions became, logically enough, stone, which skilled craftsmen were already capable of shaping practically at will for the construction of public buildings or monuments (see *Stone in Traditional Architecture* by the same author).

Thus we see appearing in Europe at this time a distinct division into zones of different cultures and mentalities between north and south. In the north, the populations lived in peasant societies where the land and forest were sacred and abounded with spirits with which it was necessary to live in harmony; in the south, on the other hand, the societies became more and more stratified, and an ever-increasing and influential part of the population lived in cities, preoccupied with activities having little or no relation with the land or the forests, and exploiting the resource of their territories in an immoderate quest for money, without regard for natural equilibriums.

North of the Mediterranean basin (in what is now Britain, north and central France, Belgium, the Netherlands, the Germanic countries, Scandinavia, and Eastern Europe), another division into zones of different building traditions also appears. In the east, Scandinavia (except for Denmark) and the Alpine and Carpathian regions preferring use tree trunks piled horizontally one upon another as described in Chapter 3. This division seems to correspond to that between the coniferous forests of the far northern or of high altitude zones, where tall, straight pines grow in great numbers, and the deciduous forests of regions with more moderate climates, where oak was the choice building material.

The tall, straight pines of the northern and high altitude forests were particularly well-suited to log construction, where the logs must touch one another (or almost) along their entire length, often more than eight or even ten meters.

For frame construction, on the other hand, even twisted pieces of only two or three meters long, which the deciduous forest furnishes more readily than long straight pieces, can be used. (See figures 14 and 15).

This chapter will deal, then, with the architectures found in the second zone, which extends (*grosso modo*, and with many zones of exception to my generalization), over the countries now known as England, France (except for the Mediterranean region), Germany, Belgium, the Netherlands, and Denmark (including the extreme south of Sweden, which was part of Denmark until 1658, and which, like Denmark, is a low-lying land where deciduous forests prevail).

Figure 14. Frame construction with daub infill, Château de Crevecoeur, Normandy, France.

Figure 15. Construction with logs, piled horizontally. Maihaugen Ethnographic Park, Lillehammer, Norway.

Figures 14 and 15. TWO DIFFERENT "FAMILIES" OF WOOD CONSTRUCTION.

Figure 16. Troyes, France

The Structure of the Frame

A basic frame, a rectangle, is nonetheless a fragile thing, which can easily be pushed askew if subjected to strong lateral forces, even when the corner joinery has been carefully done. But this can be strengthened by adding diagonal pieces and thus creating "triangular" force components, much more rigid structurally. These diagonal pieces are called *braces*.

Additional horizontal and vertical pieces, while not as effective as braces for consolidating the frame, are nonetheless useful. In fact the denser the framework, the better the structural resistance; but the denser the framework, the more wood must be cut and squared, and so the builder loses the advantage of frame construction, with its many open spaces, over log construction, where the walls are entirely of wood. The builders tried, consequently, to find optimal solutions whereby a minimum of wood provided a maximum of stability. Each territory found its own solution, so that it is usually possible (when one knows the regional styles) to tell where a house comes from simply be seeing it in a photo.

There are, then, as well as divisions into "families" of building techniques referred to earlier, sub-divisions into sub-families according to the characteristics of the frame (and these also subdivide, and so on, to the delight of ethnologists).

Figure 17. Rouen, Normandy

Figure 18. Rouen, Normandy

Figure 19. Rouen, Normandy

Figure 20. Infill material: pieces of roofing tile, Manor of Caudemone, Normandy

Figure 21. Infill material: tuffeau stone (a soft, porous, local limestone); village in the Quercy region of southwestern France.

FIGURES 18-21. CONSOLIDATION OF THE FRAMES BY USING BRACES

Figure 22. Diagonal brace; Alsatian ethnological museum, Ungersheim, France

Figure 23. Diagonal braces; Alsatian ethnological museum, Ungersheim, France

Figure 24. Principal framework of large posts with enlarged, decorated upper ends. Rouen, Normandy, France

Figure 25. The principal framework of large timbers can be easily distinguished from the secondary framework of smaller pieces placed between the principal posts. Pont l'Evêque, Normandy

To deal only with the major subdivisions, we can distinguish the Norman frame (carried from Normandy into England, and also spreading eastward and southward through France) from the Germanic framework, with the line a separation running along the crest of the Vosges mountains in eastern France. (Please note that this is not the border between modern France and modern Germany. The region of Alsace, from which I have taken many examples of the Germanic framework, lies east of the Vosges and is now part of France – since 1648, with the exception of those periods when Germany took it back militarily for a time before losing it again. But until that date, Alsace was part of a Germanic cultural zone, and was, all through the Middle Ages, politically a part of one or another league of Germanic states. Even after union with France, it retained many of its regional particularities, including language, and has to this day.)

To the west of this demarcation line, especially in Normandy, we find a very evident "principal" framework characterized by stout posts at the corners and at intervals along the façade. These go from the ground level (or more usually, from a stone footing) up to the first story height, where they enlarge into a decorative base (almost like a "capital" in medieval church architecture), which supports an overhang, or *jetty*, of the story above. (See figure 24.) This widening of the post (the tree would be turned upside down, so the thicker bottom could provide the volume necessary for this enlargement) is often marked with moldings or other decorative effects, which may include sculpture in the most refined works. Between these principal posts is added a secondary structure of thinner pieces.

Figures 26-27. Principal framework of large posts with enlarged, decorated upper ends. Rouen, Normandy.

Figures 28-29. Troyes, Champagne region, France

In the old city of Troyes in the Champagne region of France, the French style of principal and secondary frameworks is used, as in Normandy. Here, however, the principal pillars are not reduced through their length to leave an enlarged upper section; rather, a supporting brace is added, and assembled to the pillar with mortise and tenon joints, a technique which will be explained further on in this chapter.

Figure 30. Manor of Orbec, Normandy

Figure 31. Manor of Aubichon, Normandy

Figure 32. Colmar, Alsace

Figure 33. Alsatian ethnological museum, Ungersheim.

Figures 34. Braces in a "man" design, frequent in Germanic framework; Colmar, Alsace.

In the Germanic frame, on the other hand, the uprights are spaced much further apart, and we can see that one or two horizontal beams have been added at mid-level (or at the one-third and the two-thirds levels) of each story. These have a considerable consolidating effect. A further consolidating factor is the generous use (compared to the Norman frame) of long braces. These diagonal pieces are often treated in a decorative manner east of the Vosges Mountains, and their joining patterns are part of the repertory and the vocabulary of the Germanic carpenter. Thus, we often find the *man* (*mann* in German and in Alsatian) as shown on these pages, with possible regional variations.

Figure 35. Braces in a "man" design, frequent in Germanic framework; Colmar, Alsace.

Figure 36. Note the use here of the early technique of "long posts" (generally abandoned after the seventeenth century), where posts and braces of a single piece each run through two, or sometimes even three, stories. Alsatian ethnological museum, Ungersheim, Alsace

Figure 37. Alsatian ethnological museum

Figure 38. "Little Venice" (because of its many canals), the old tanners quarter; Colmar, Alsace.

Figure 39. Canton Thurgau, Switzerland

Figure 40. Bad Urach, in the Schwabische Jura, Germany

FIGURES 39-41. OTHER EXAMPLES OF GERMANIC "FACHWERK" (FRAME CONSTRUCTION)

Figure 41. Rothenburg ob der Tauber, Germany

Figure 42. Farmhouse from eastern Jutland, Denmark, now in the Danish Open Air Museum, Lyngby.

Further to the east and the north, the framework shows a combination of the characteristics of those described above; we can see in these photos, from Denmark, that the posts are spaced widely apart, as in Alsace, but that the frame contains relatively few braces, as in the French, or Norman, frame. This is partly due to regional particularities, but also to the long, low form of the Danish farmhouse.

Figure 43. Farm from Scania, southern Sweden (formerly part of Denmark); now in the Danish Open Air Museum, Lyngby.

Figure 44. Farmhouse from eastern Jutland, Denmark, now in the Danish Open Air Museum, Lyngby.

Figure 45. Urban house and workshops from the eighteenth century. Aarhus, Den Gamle By (The Old Town), open air museum of urban architecture.

Figure 46. Farm from Seeland, Denmark, now in the Danish Open Air Museum, Lyngby.

Figure 47. Farmhouse from western Jutland, Denmark, now in the Danish Open Air Museum, Lyngby.

Figure 48. Rouen, Normandy

Figure 49. Rouen, Normandy

Figure 50. Rouen, Normandy. Notice the use of the curved beam and how the structure of the frame is adapted to it.

DIFFERENT PATTERNS IN THE USE OF SMALL BRACES

In Normandy, although it is not rare to see braces extending through one full story, the most common form of diagonal reinforcement is by the use of shorter pieces set in underneath the window frames in cross patterns. (See figures 50 - 54.)

Figure 51. Rouen, Normandy

Figure 52. Orbec Manor, Normandy

Figure 53. Rouen, Normandy

Figure 54. Rouen, Normandy

Figure 55. Turckheim, Alsace

Figures 55-56. Crossed braces beneath the window frames are less common in Alsace than in Normandy, but when they are used, they are often shaped or sculpted for a decorative effect.

Figure 56. Turckheim, Alsace

Figure 57. Aarhus, Den Gamle By (The Old Town), open air museum of urban architecture

Figure 58. Køge, Denmark

Figures 57-58. In Danish urban architecture, the use of short braces set under the window frames is also common. Here, however, although they may be placed in a cross pattern, they are most often set in a "man" design.

Figure 59. Rural Normandy

Figures 59-62. As opposed to urban practices in architecture, rural houses and outbuildings in Normandy tend to have their braces placed, several together, in the corners formed by a post and the foundation sill.

Figure 60. Rural Normandy

Figure 61. Rural Normandy

Figure 62. Rural Normandy

Joinery

In prehistoric times, as related above, builders had already understood that to place a horizontal beam upon vertical posts, it was necessary to find a way of fixing the pieces in place. Throughout the neolithic period, the solutions commonly used were:

1) to cut a rounded groove into the top of the post to better receive the horizontal beam,

2) to use a natural fork in the tree as the upper end of the post receiving the beam.

Figures 63-65. All these photos were taken at the Beynac Archeological Park, France.

At the same period, the more inventive builders saw that it was also possible to trim the end of the beam inserted into the fork for a better adjustment, and that one could also drill a hole through the two pieces and insert a wooden peg, or *dowel,* to hold them together, as shown in the photo.

By extending such reasoning, builders also discovered that they could do without the fork by piercing a hole in the post and by inserting the end of the horizontal beam, which could then be fixed in place with a dowel (wooden pin). It was this innovation that allowed the development of frame construction: the hole (generally rectangular) cut to receive the piece is called a *mortise*, and the end of the piece to be inserted, which is cut to a somewhat reduced section, is called a *tenon* (from the French, *mortaise et tenon*).

Researchers in the field of protohistory have found such joinery techniques in the remains of neolithic structures, but they were less common than more rudimentary techniques, probably because making a mortise required tools that took a long time to fabricate, at that period.

As the method for making such joints is explained in the technical section (*The Carpenter's Handbook*), the accompanying diagram (figure 66) will suffice at this point. This type of joinery is also used with diagonal braces, as shown in *figure 67*. Detailed indications for assembling the pieces are given in *The Carpenter's Handbook.*

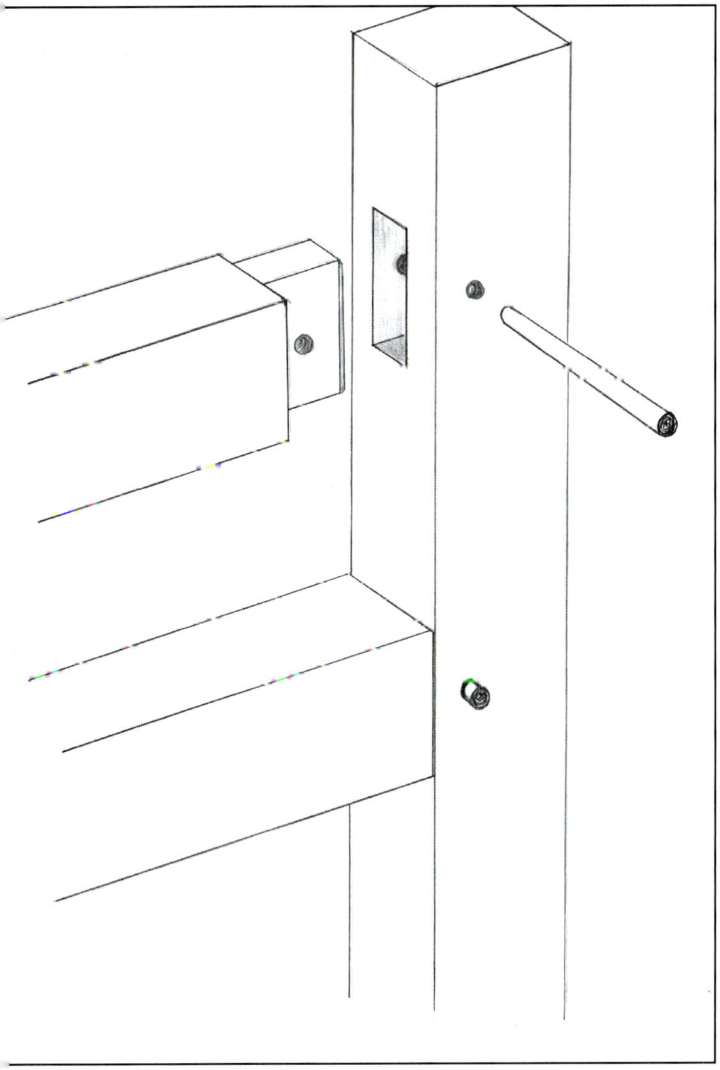

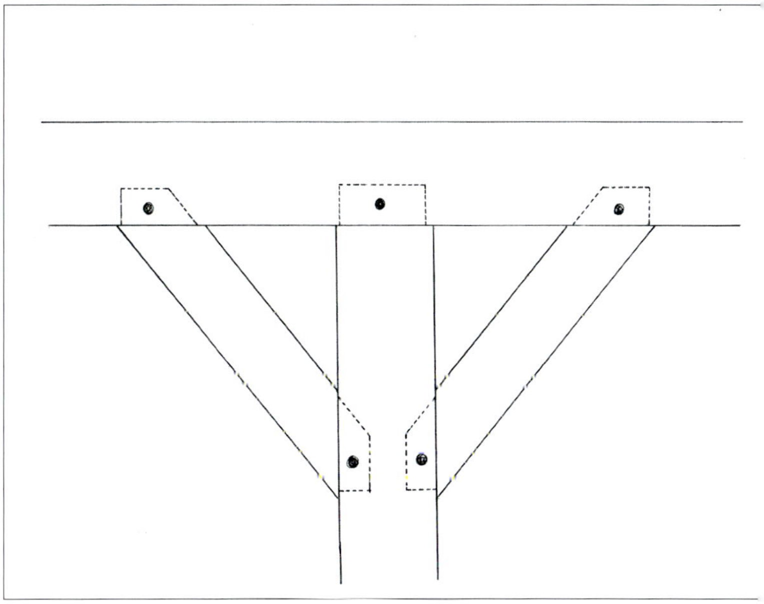

Figures 66 & 67.

As more efficient tools were developed with the advent of bronze and then iron working, further innovations were developed. To improve the joinery, the use of round logs was gradually and generally abandoned in favour of squared logs (see *The Carpenter's Handbook* for the methods of squaring), which the new iron tools could shape much more readily than before. Chisels of all sizes, gouges of all curves, specialized axes for hewing, adzes, drawknives and planes for smoothing, awls and drills for piercing dowel-holes, were all developed. The increasing variety and complexity of the tools led to an increasing variety and complexity in the joining techniques. This in turn led to greater stability and also allowed for a better junction of several pieces at one point, a necessity for building supplementary stories.

Equally important, the development of increasingly stratified societies led to the emergence of a class of building specialists at the service of the more wealthy. In the Middle Ages, these artisans grouped together into "crafts guilds," or associations of workers of the same craft. Competition between guilds, but also the desire of the individual craftsman to be recognized by his peers and to excel in his domain, also led to a flowering of both technical prowess and decorative effects, which are shown further on in this chapter.

Figure 69. Wattle infill of pliable branches, Alsatian Open Air Museum.

Figure 68. Alsatian Open Air Museum, Ungersheim

Figure 70. Wattle infill of split branches, partially rendered with a clay "daub" mixture; Alsatian Ope Air Museum.

Filling in the Frame

The frame is conceived to be self-supporting and to carry the weight of the roof as well. It was first drawn, and later assembled — after the individual pieces had been cut and notched to correspond to the plan — on a flat and level working space. This might be done on the building site, but could also be done in a workshop with enough space to trace and assemble an entire wall at full scale, the pieces being transported later to the building site. As can be seen from the accompanying photo of a framework without infill (from the Alsatian open air museum), it stands alone and carries the substantial weight of a clay-tiled roof. The infill is added only to enclose the space and insulate it to keep in the heat produced by fires — and later by stoves and ovens — but has little structural function. The traditions established by the Neolithic communities throughout Europe as early as several thousand years before Christ were basically maintained throughout the Middle Ages and right up until modern times (late nineteenth or early twentieth century). Branches were wedged by force into grooves cut on the inside of the members of the framework; other, more supple, branches were interwoven with these, and the resulting "wattle" support copiously rendered with a "daub" mixture applied from both sides.

Figure 71. The earth mixture can be hand formed into balls and inserted between vertical infill branches, and then rendered over; Alsatian Open Air Museum, Ungersheim.

Figure 72. When the uprights are set close together, as is often the case in Normandy, the daub mixture can be applied to a support of short sticks wedged diagonally in a zigzag pattern between the uprights.

Figure 73. Alsatian Open Air Museum, Ungersheim, Alsace

Figure 75. Crèvecoeur Castle, Normandy

Figure 74. Alsatian Open Air Museum, Ungersheim, Alsace

Figure 76. Beynac Archeological Park, Dordogne

Figures 73 – 76. A variety of renderings and surface coats are possible: the daub can be smoothed with the palms of the hand, or with a trowel or a board, or by rubbing with a piece of sheepskin. The application of additional finer layers of daub mortar will give a smoother finish. The surface can be drawn on with a stick or with the fingers, or whitewashed with lime or kaolin clay, or painted with mixtures containing pigments.

Figure 77. Finish coat of lime mortar. Alsatian Open Air Museum

Figures 77-78. In the Middle Ages and later, the daub was often rendered with a coat of lime mortar or with plaster. This became standard practice in towns and cities, moreover, to the point of entirely supplanting the use of earth mixtures.

Figure 78. Daub infill with a finish coat of lime mortar, partly fallen off after several decades of disrepair; farm building in Normandy. Notice the supporting infill of sticks placed in a zigzag pattern.

Figure 79. Restoration project in the city of Troyes, France.

Figure 80. Restoration project in the city of Troyes, France.

As we have seen at the Beynac Archeological Park, the frame buildings of Neolithic times were completely covered over with mud mortar. It was only when the skilled craftsmen of the Middle Ages were perfecting their art that the practice of leaving the frame structure visible became general, and only the infilled panels were covered with mortar. But often city ordinances (such as that of Paris in 1607), intending to limit the spread of fires, decreed that wooden frame structures be covered over with plaster. Apart from safety concerns, moreover, in following centuries, the bourgeoisie, disdaining wood as being worthy of peasants only, tended to have their wood frame houses completely plastered over. This was done by nailing on thin wooden lathing to hold the plaster or lime mortar, traces of which can be seen on the uprights in the accompanying photos. The resulting facades would be painted over (sometimes even with imitation masonry joints) and were quasi-indistinguishable from masonry buildings.

At the present time, if it was not already done sooner, the trend is to restore these houses to their original state — at least above the ground floor, often occupied by shops which have created modern window displays.

Figure 81. Recent restorations in the city of Troyes, France.

Figure 82. Colmar, Alsace

Figure 83. Cahors, southwest France

Jettied Upper Stories

As medieval cities grew rapidly, legislation soon came into being defining and restricting the space on the ground available for houses. In response, the builders built cantilevered upper stories, each level projecting outward from the one below, by simply extending the floor joists of each upper story (in the direction of the run of the joists, of course. In the transversal directions, it was much more difficult, and hence less commonly practiced. Short extension beams had to spring perpendicularly from the joists to form the lateral overhang, and had to be very solidly tied in so as to be able to support the weight placed on them). There were, of course, limits to respect, so that the upper story would not be overbalanced (especially if many people gathered at the windows of the overhanging facade); a slight cantilever of 30or 40 cm. was stable enough, but for more, it was best to reinforce the overhanging joists with braces springing from the wall below. For an overhang of more than one metre, the joists had to be supported by vertical posts placed on the ground, which thus created a covered passageway. These can be seen around many village market squares; in more restrained spaces, it was not normally possible to place posts or pillars in or across the street.

Figure 84. Covered passageway in Réalville, southwest France.

Figure 85. Colmar, Alsace, France

Figure 86. The Old Town (den Gamle By), Aarhus, Denmark.

The sixteenth century marked the height of developement of this style of building, as rich merchants and city officials competed to build prestigious dwellings; building craftsmen consequently had great scope for developing and expressing their own creativity and mastery (within the limits of an established style). This was the case everywhere in the towns of northwestern and central Europe, from the Langeudoc (southwestern France) to southern Sweden via England or the Germanic states. But this building fervour progressively diminished, and by the eighteenth century, practically all new frame buildings were greatly simplified works. Although they could rise to three or four stories in height, their facades were constructed in a single, vertical plane, using wood of more modest dimensions with few moldings or sculptures.

Figure 87. The Old Town (den Gamle By), Aarhus, Denmark.

Figure 88. Rouen, Normandy

In Normandy, and especially in Rouen, there are many "mullioned" windows, a style much used in Renaissance architecture—be it in stone or in wood. (See also figures 25, 26, 27, and 51.) These windows are composed of multiple panels separated by vertical end horizontal frame elements, often carved. The standard module, in most Renaissance architecture, is four panels per window (two upper and two lower), but there can be any multiple of two. Here, the multiplication of sets of windows makes for a facade that is mostly glass. The wood frame structure lends itself perfectly to this practice, as glass can replace the usual opaque infill panels, which are not structural elements, the frame alone filling this function. (Refer back to page 50.)

Figure 89. Rouen, Normandy

Figure 90. Normandy

Figure 91. Normandy

Figure 92. Southern Sweden

In the Renaissance manors and townhouses of Normandy, the space created by the jettying of the story is covered, on the facade, by highly decorated beams which are assembled with the posts of the principal framework. These are usually carved with a complex molding running the length of the beam. In many cases the lines of the molding curve to converge to a point at or just before touching the intervening posts, or disappear into the jaws of a beast carved into the beam. This is a regional particularity of Normandy, shared, in France, only with neighboring Brittany. Yet, a very similar manner of treating this space also appears in Denmark and in southern Sweden.

Figure 93. Normandy

Figure 94. Normandy

Figure 95. Denmark

Chapter 3
Log Construction

Figure 96

Assembling the Logs

Unlike the system of frame construction described in the preceding pages, where the builder creates wooden frames with much space between the elements which is filled with some other material, in this system, logs are piled one on top of the other, horizontally, to construct walls entirely of wood. Whereas frame construction is characterized by the use of many vertical pieces, log construction is characterized by the predominance of horizontal elements. Because of the rectilinear nature of logs, they are most easily used to construct rectangular buildings, although octagons are often found, as in the bell-towers of Russian churches (see the title page of this chapter), and any multi-sided figure is possible.

If we imagine early builders experimenting with log construction, we can see the multiple problems which arise, and the multitude of possible solutions which can be found.

Let us imagine then, that the early builders have seen that they can build up in height by piling logs in parallel pairs, perpendicular to and resting upon, another parallel pair (fig. 1 and 1a).

The first problem is that the logs will roll, and thus the pile is very unstable. Possible solutions are:

cut a notch (called a "saddle notch") in the supporting log to receive the log which will be placed upon it (2 and 2a), or

square the logs (or simply their ends, where one log rests upon another) to have flat surfaces resting on flat surfaces (3 and 3a).

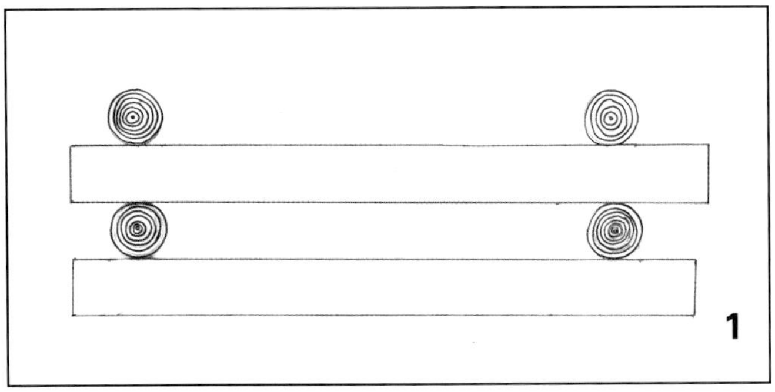

Figure 97

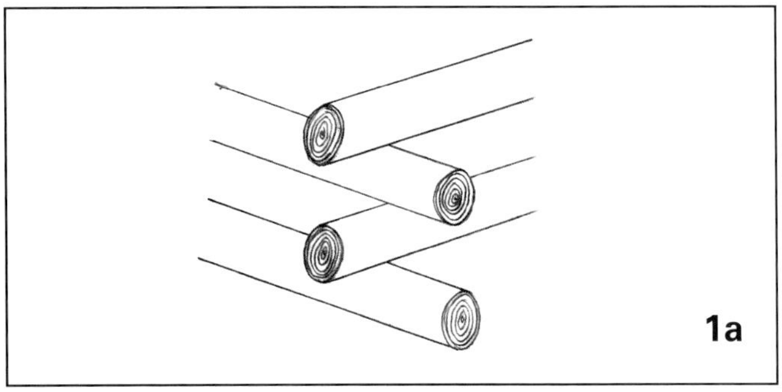

Figure 98

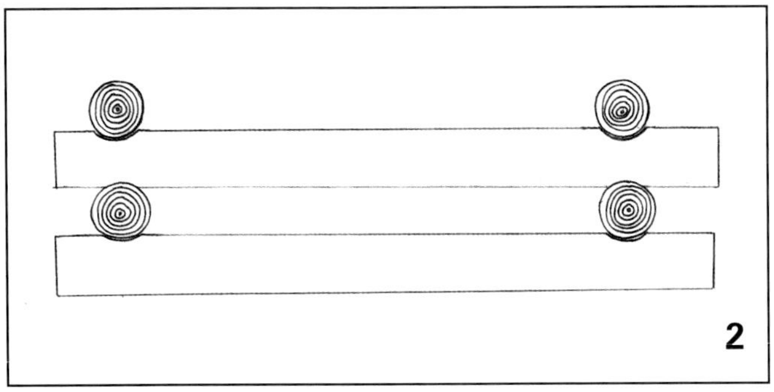

Figure 99

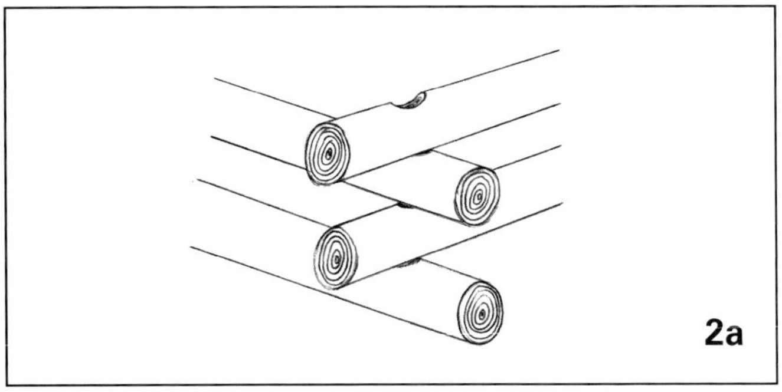

Figure 100

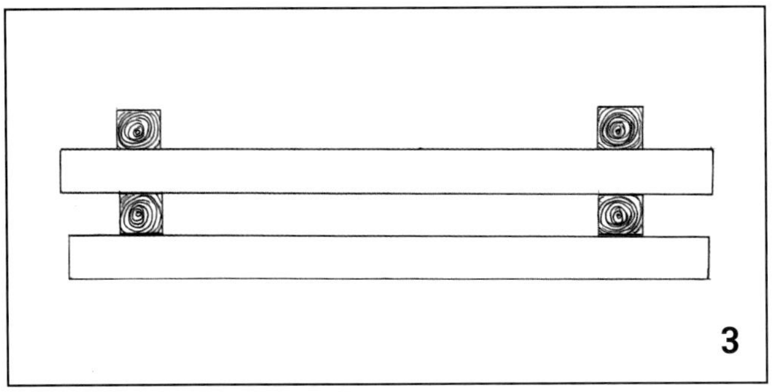

Figure 101

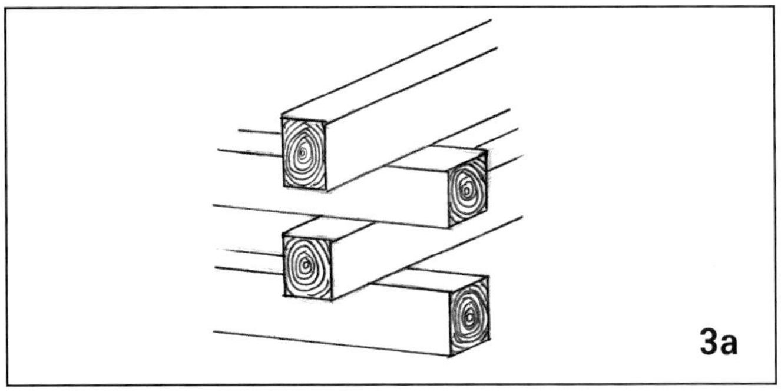

Figure 102

Figure 103. Small church from the region of Lake Onega in the republic of Carelia, Russia; now in the Kizhi Museum of Wooden Architecture, Kizhi Island, Russia.

To achieve still greater stability, the notches (called *saddle notches* in round logs, *lap joints* in squared logs) can be cut deeper – about halfway through the log (4 and 4a). This provides better resistance to movement. At the same time, as the upper log descends further into the supporting logs, it drops down to touch the parallel log below it, so there is no big gap between the logs for wind and rain to come through.

Nonetheless, when we are dealing with round logs, the thermal efficiency of such a wall remains very poor, as at the joints the thickness of the wall is zero, and the joints are thus prone to losing the heat produced inside the house. So, the notches can be cut a bit deeper still, to lower each log further, and a groove is cut in the lower part of each log so that it rests upon the supporting log as shown (5 and 5a). The method is given in detail in *The Carpenter's Handbook* (p 166).

The thickness of the wall is thus only slightly reduced at the joint, and now has a better thermal efficiency.

To further improve this thermal efficiency, whatever sort of vegetal fiber is readily available (moss, straw, flax, hemp, or linseed fibers) can be used as insulator to fill the joints, compacting as necessary to fill any irregularities.

When squared logs are used, they are assembled with *lap* (*overlapping*) *joints* cut halfway through one of the logs or one quarter of the way through both logs (6 and 6a). These are easier to trace than the round notches, as we are dealing here with straight cuts. This system is also explained in *The Carpenter's Handbook*, on page 166.

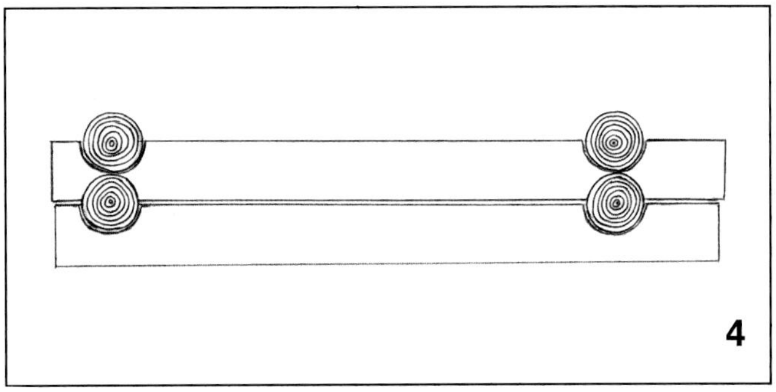

Figure 104

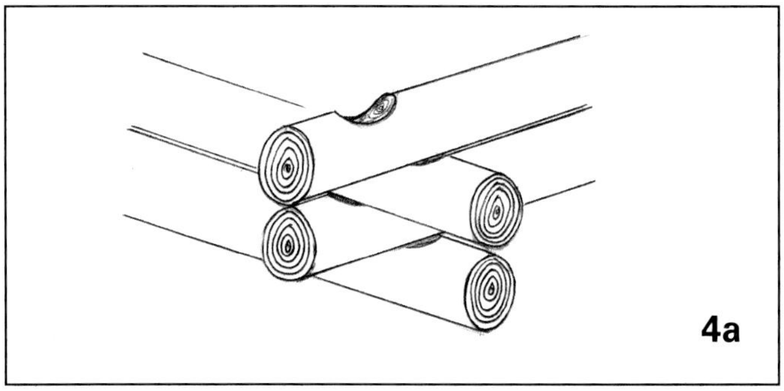

Figure 105

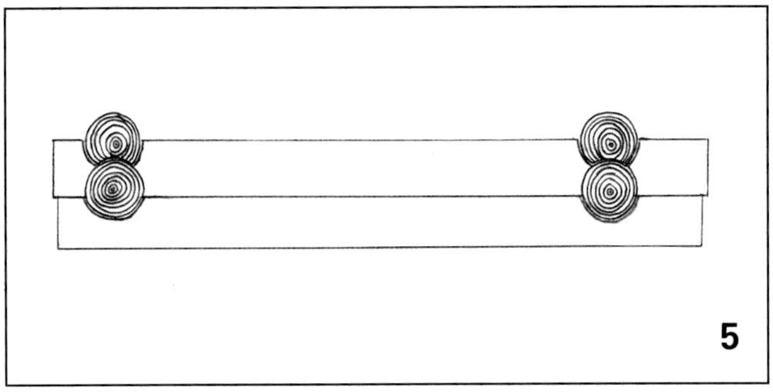

Figure 106

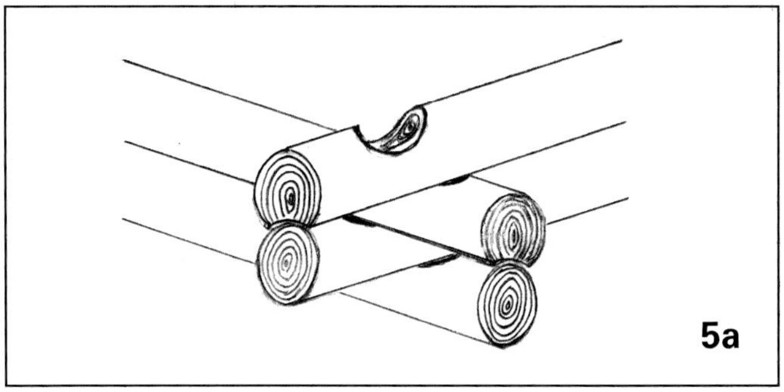

Figure 107

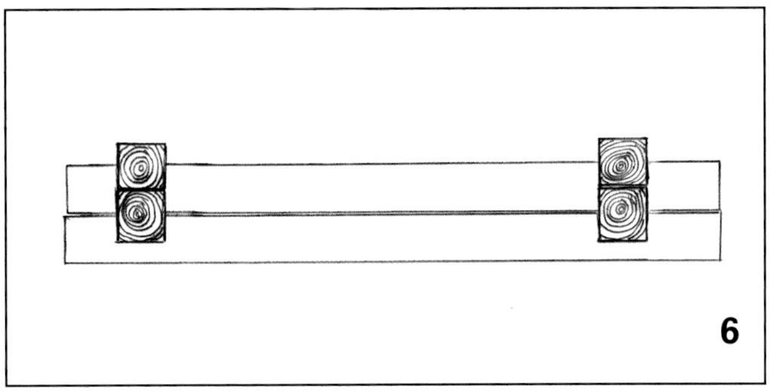

Figure 108

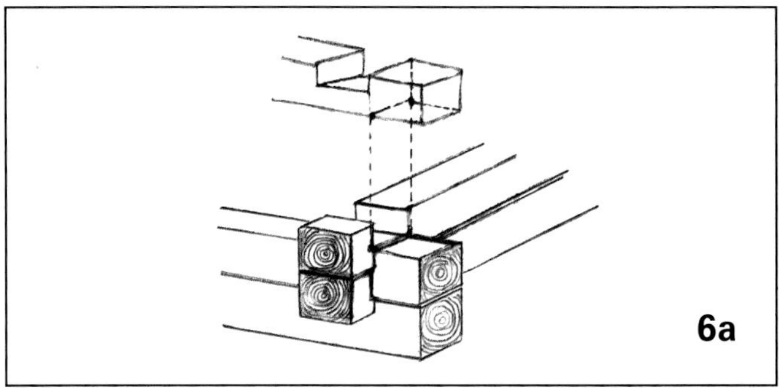

Figure 109

Figure 110. Round logs assembled using round notches. We can see, on the log ends, that a rounded groove is cut on the underside of each log to allow it to sit better on the log below, closing the joint between the two tightly. Vitoslavlitsy Ethnographic Museum, Novgorod, Russia.

Figure 111. Each of the logs to be assembled is notched above and below through about 1/4 of its height.

Figure 112. Here, each of the logs to assemble is notched through about 1/3 of its height on the top, and about 1/6 of its height underneath.

In northwest Russia, the logs are traditionally used round and assembled with round 1/4 or 1/2 notches, as here (Figure 111), or with some variant such as that shown Figure 112. Traditionally, the logs should be notches and grooves are cut out with an axe (see *The Carpenter's Handbook* for the method). The log ends are also cut with the axe (where the tradition is maintained); this closes the wood's fibers against humidity and insects, contributing to the longevity of the building, whereas cutting with a saw leaves the fibers open to penetration and decomposition. Cutting through the log with V-cuts takes several minutes more than sawing it manually; and with a further five to ten minutes of application, one can hew the log's end flat in the vertical plane.

Normally, the notches fit more tightly than in these photos; I have chosen these examples because their very imprecision allows us to see clearly how the notches overlap. When the joint is tight, as was probably the case before retraction of the wood, it is difficult to distinguish which log has been notched, and to what depth. These variants can be used both with squared logs and with round logs (see photos).

Figures 113-114. Granaries, Kizhi Museum of Wooden Architecture, Russia.

Logs used round in the tradition of north-west Russia

Figure 115. Kizhi Museum of Wooden Architecture, Russia.

Figure 116. Kizhi Museum of Wooden Architecture, Russia.

Figures 117-119. Houses of prosperous peasants from the shores of Lake Onega, Russia, nineteenth century; now in the Kizhi Museum of Wooden Architecture, Russia. In these well-crafted houses, the logs have been hewed where they form the inside walls of the living or sleeping rooms, to give straight walls with smooth surfaces.

Figure 120. Excepting the granary (to the left) and the bathhouse (to the right), all the functions of the farm (living quarters, stables, storerooms, and workshops) are grouped under the same vast roof. Kizhi Museum of Wooden Architecture, Russia.

In many other countries, the logs are usually squared by hewing with an axe (see *Carpentry Techniques of Olden Times* for the method). There are several possible variants:

The logs can be "perfectly squared" by cutting to the dimensions of a square, which can be fitted entirely inside the diameter of the round log: The angles of the resulting squared log will be sharp through its entire length (fig.1).

Figure 121.

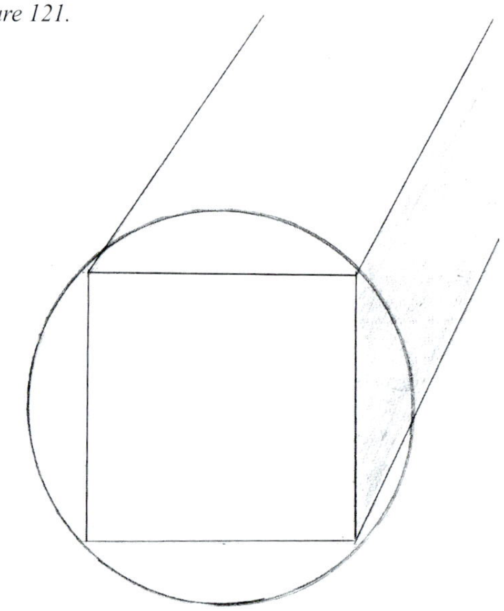

More often than not, though, to obtain bigger cross-sections, the square will slightly exceed the limits of the circular log, and the resulting angles will be rounded and irregular (as the log is itself somewhat irregular and not a perfect cylinder) (fig.2).

Figure 122.

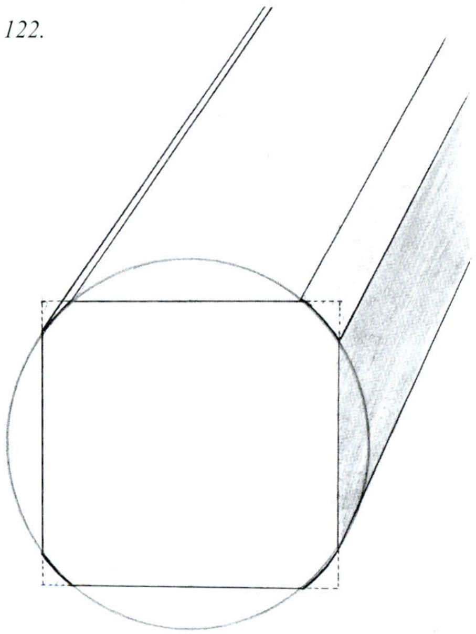

Figure 123. Detail of house from the Gudbrandsdal, Norway; now in the Maihaugen Ethnographic Museum, Lillehammer.

Figure 123-a. House from the Gudbrandsdal, Norway; now in the Maihaugen Ethnographic Museum, Lillehammer.

Figure 124. Quarter lap joint; church from the Biesczady Mountains of Poland; now in the Sanok ethnographic park, Sanok, Poland.

Sometimes, (for example, in the churches of the Carpathian Mountains in Poland and in Slovakia), the trees used are of very large diameter, and each tree is cut in half to give two rectangular-section logs. These logs have sharp angles on the inside, and these are placed on the inside of the edifice to form a perfectly fitted surface (which often serves as a support for decorative painting directly on the walls). The outside, rounded angles are turned toward the outside of the structure.

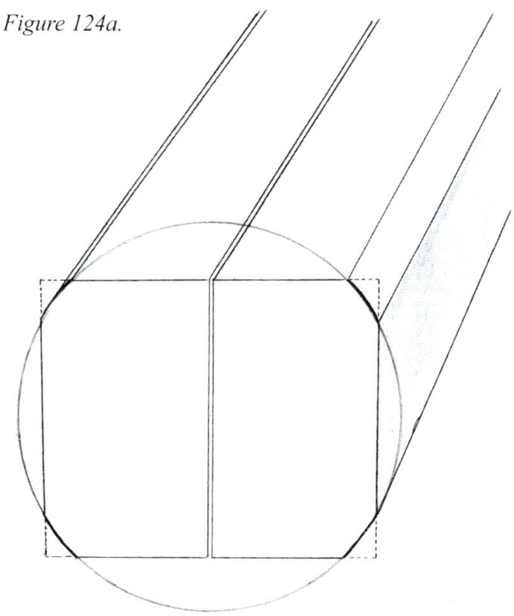

Figure 124a.

Figure 125. Dovetail joints; Stara Lubovna ethnological park, Slovakia.

A more elaborate type of joint, also used since Neolithic times, is the "dovetail," where the log ends are cut, both on their top and bottom sides, to slope in two directions. These sloping ends are perfectly adjusted with their perpendicular partners, also cut with similar but opposite and complementary slopes, which wedge against one another in such a way that no movement is possible in any direction.

Figure 126. Dovetail joints; Bardejov ethnological park, Slovakia.

Figures 127-128. Wallachian ethnomuseum, Rožnov pod Radhoštem, Czeckia

Figures 129-130. Granary in Savoy, France.

Figures 131-132. Farm buildings from the Setesdal, Norway; now in the Norsk Folkemuseum, Oslo.

Another possible way to hew the logs, much used in Norway: to an oval form.

Figures 133-134. Maihaugen open-air museum, Lillehammer, Norway.

In Norway, round or oval logs are often hewed to a hexagonal form at their ends, with varying degrees of precision. This form allows the carpenter to adjust flat surfaces against flat surfaces at the corners. The oblique cuts that fit against one another can be seen, or guessed at, in the photos of Figures 135-138, taken in different parts of Norway.

Figures 135-138. Corner joinery from different parts of Norway. Inside the joint, there are usually interlocking notches whose precise form varies with the region and the period.

Figure 139. Building under construction near Zakopane, Poland. The shims (wooden blocks) will be removed once the fiber insulation has been inserted between the logs, which will then descend to compact the fibers for a tight fit.

Figure 140. Wooden peg visible in the wall of a log house, Novy Sacs ethnomuseum, Poland.

Figure 141. Holding the logs in place by the use of a pair of vertical posts. Savoy, France. (The other post of the pair is on the inside of the wall; together, they "sandwich" the wall logs.)

Holding the Logs in Place

Although good corner joints (lap joints, saddle notches, or dovetail joints) give considerable stability to a structure by prohibiting movement of the individual logs under normal conditions of stress, further assurance of stability can be gained by pegging, or pinning, each log into the one below it with a thick wooden pin. This is particularly useful in places where a log has been cut for a door or window frame, and therefore does not join a perpendicular log to form a corner.

In addition, when interior partition walls are tied into the outer walls, they help reinforce them. When there are no interior walls, or if these are very far apart, a further system for reinforcing the logs is often used in Savoy (alpine France). This consists of a pair of vertical posts, one on each side of the wall, assembled with a floor joist or some other structural element of the building, which can be prolonged to pass through the wall.

Figures 142-143. Hay barn, Bardejov ethnographic park, Slovakia

Insulating the Joints

The building shown here is a barn for storing hay, where ventilation is desirable; consequently, what would be considered faulty construction in a house is good construction for this intended purpose. The walls are made of irregular logs, which it would be difficult to use for precision building; here, then, is a use for an abundant local resource, and the farmer can conserve his stock of quality logs for more demanding building projects. Note the use of roughly cut dovetail joints, evidence of a certain degree of technical proficiency in spite of the haphazard appearance.

Figures 144-145. Bardejov ethnographic park, Slovakia

In this building, also of irregular and consequently ill-fitting logs, the large spaces between the members are filled with clay. When this is done, the spaces are usually first filled roughly by wedging in branches or saplings, whole or split, which will fill most of the space and allow the mud mortar to adhere better.

Figures 146-147. Bardejov ethnographic park, Slovakia

Here, the infill is of earth mixed with straw, a mixture which does not crack as much as clay upon drying.

A lime wash (colored with blue pigment) has been passed over the whole structure, for decoration, disinfection, and protection. Normally, it would be renewed annually to prevent its flaking off.

Note here also the ceiling, where the logs form a rounded barrel vault. The roof is simply poised above this, resting on a couple of the sidewall's logs, which overhang the facade.

Figure 148. Sanok ethnomuseum, Poland; a house of the Bojki ethnic group, Carpathian Mountain people speaking a Ukrainian dialect. These peoples migrated along the Carpathian chain during several centuries, and by the beginning of the twentieth century were settled in the territories that are now part of Poland, Ukrainia, and Slovakia.

Figures 148-149. This procedure of filling the joints with earth (or lime mortar, or plaster) and whitewashing or painting the infill thus becomes part of the aesthetics of the building.

Figure 149. Museum of Ukrainian Culture, Svidnik, Slovakia, a museum dedicated to the "Ruthenian" ethnic group, speaking a Ukrainian dialect.

Figure 150. Museum of Ukrainian Culture, Svidnik, Slovakia

Figure 151. Wallachian Ethnomuseum, Rožnov pod Radhoštem, Czeckia

Figures 150-153. THE MAIN LIVING (AND COOKING AND SLEEPING) ROOM IN EASTERN EUROPEAN PEASANT HOUSES

Many of the interiors of Eastern European peasant houses are entirely whitewashed – the logs as well as the infill – and in some areas (the valleys around Sanok in southeast Poland, for example), the outside may also be whitewashed, as in the following pages.

Figure 152. Novy Sacz Ethnographic Park, Poland

Figure 153. Sanok Ethnographic Park, Poland

Figure 154. Novy Sacz Ethnographic Park, Poland

FIGURES 154-156. PEASANT HOUSES FROM THE HILL AND VALLEY AREAS OF SOUTHWEST POLAND.

Figure 155. Sanok Ethnographic Park, Poland

Figure 156. Sanok Ethnographic Park, Poland

Figure 157. A clay rendering painted over with lime whitewash covers the living part of this Ukrainian peasant house; now in the Museum of Folk Life and Architecture of the Ukraine, Kiev.

In certain areas of Eastern Europe (parts of Moldavia and Transylvania in Romania; much of eastern Ukraine), log houses were often rendered with a coat of daub. This could vary in thickness from a thin layer, which left the contours of the logs visible, to a very thick layer meant to give the walls a smooth, straight finish. This practice was most often limited to the living quarters of the farmhouse—the barns, stables, and workshops being left uncovered. The daub coating was then painted (usually with a white lime wash) and often decorated with some lines or designs of pigmented clay.

As the daub does not stick to smooth wooden surfaces, these surfaces had to be prepared to receive the mortar. This could be done by driving small wooden wedges into cracks in the logs (at about 20 cm. intervals). Otherwise, the house could be completely covered with a latticework of thin wood. When this was done, the only visible evidence that the house is made of logs are observed at the protruding corners where the logs cross, which may or may not be covered. (See the facing and the following pages.)

Figure 158. Clay-rendered, whitewashed house from Transylvania, Romania, now in the Village Open Air Museum, Bucharest.

Figure 159. Novy Sacz Ethnographic Park, Poland

Figures 159-160. TWO WAYS OF PREPARING A LOG WALL TO RECEIVE A COAT OF RENDERING.

Above right: on small wooden wedges forced into cracks in the wood. Below right: on thin wooden battens nailed onto the wooden surface.

Figure 160. The Village Open Air Museum, Bucharest

Figure 161. Museum of Ukrainian Folk Life and Architecture, Kiev

Figure 162. Museum of Ukrainian Folk Life and Architecture, Kiev

The rendering can be done with varying degrees of refinement; compare the treatment of this house with that shown in figure 163.

Figure 163. House from the Bucovina region of the Ukraine, bordering on Romania. Now in the Museum of Ukrainian Folk Life and Architecture, Kiev.

Figure 164. Museum of Ukrainian Folk Life and Architecture, Kiev

Figure 165. Museum of Ukrainian Folk Life and Architecture, Kiev

Figure 166. Stara Lubovna Ethnographic Park, Slovakia

Figure 167. Near Zakopane, Poland

Figure 168. Near Zakopane, Poland

The best insulation, though, is a filling of vegetal fibers tightly packed into the joints, or compressed by the lowering of one log upon another. A daub mortar can be applied on top of this, if desired, mostly for reasons of aesthetics and cleanliness. A fiber filling is generally used, then, in all buildings that are intended to keep warmth in and cold out (houses, workshops, and some storage rooms) in all countries of temperate climate. Different kinds of materials are used in different areas, though, depending on what is readily available: moss, from the forest, or fibers from cultivated crops such as flax or hemp, or shavings from woodworking.

In the area around Zakopane in the Tatra Mountains of Poland, ribbon-like wood shavings (taken off with a drawknife) are often used for insulation, bunched into balls for decorative effect, as in these photos (at RIGHT).

Figure 169. Near Zakopane, Poland

Figures 170-171. Shepherd's hut and sheep-pen at the foot of the Tatra Mountains in southern Poland.

Doors and Windows

A doorway in its simplest expression

This building serves only as a mountain hut for shepherds in summer pastures in the Tatra Mountains of Poland, hence its rusticity. The doorposts, cut from logs left round, are just barely cut into the sill (bottom log) so as not to weaken this important structural piece.

The uprights (jambs) are cut into, along their length, to form a groove about 4- 6 cm. wide. Into this groove is fitted a corresponding "tongue," or *tenon*, made in each of the horizontal logs, which have been interrupted (i.e. cut) for the doorway. (This can best be seen on the right side, where the fitting is not tight.) The lintel is simply the log above the opening, a log running the full length of the building. This fitting of the horizontal logs into the uprights, which are themselves fitted into the sill and the lintel, maintains the interrupted logs in their place. (But it's best to also peg them into place, as explained above.)

Figure 172. Sanok Ethnographic Park, Poland

Figure 173. Sanok Ethnographic Park, Poland

Figures 172-173. SIMPLE WINDOW FRAMES

Figure 174. Carriage-entrance to a barn in a Russian farmhouse, where the agricultural, artisanal, and dwelling spaces are all grouped in one building. Here the lintel log has also been hewed to complete the arch begun by the two side diagonal braces, and a similar sculptural design is also carved out of each of these three elements for decoration. As on the preceding page, the lintel is not a separate piece, but rather a wall log running the entire length of the building. Kizhi Museum of Wooden Architecture, Karelia, Russia

Figure 176. A similar construction is much used in and around Zakopane, in the Tatra Mountains of Poland, where it can become quite complex. Note the shape given the diagonal braces where they are fitted into the jambs and lintel, and also the decorative use of wooden pegs.

Figure 175. Diagonal braces are cut into the jambs and the separate lintel of this doorway to a Carpathian mountain church. The braces add to the stability of the doorframe, but this is not really a necessity—probably more a decorative element, allowing the creation of an arched entranceway. (Bojki ethnic group sector of the Sanok Ethnographic Park, Poland)

Figure 177. Carefully hewn and meticulously sculpted jambs to a doorway in a **loft** *(granary/storeroom) in the Numendal, Norway. Note the curve hewed into the lintel to form an arch. Here, as in the doorway pictured in figure 174 above, the lintel is simply one of the wall logs.*

FIGURES 174-177. MORE SOPHISTICATED DOOR FRAMES

Figures 178-179. Double doorway (foreground: entrance to the veranda; background: doorway to the house) in the Carpathian region of Ukraine. Now in the Museum of Ukrainian Folk Life and Architecture, Kiev.

Figures 180-181. Latvian Ethnographic Park, Riga

Verandas and Balconies

This Latvian peasant house, with its arcaded porch, illustrates the co-existence of log with post-and-beam construction. The house is visibly built of logs (squared) set one upon the other, and the door frame is solidly connected with the wall logs by tongue and groove joinery, as is described in the preceding pages of this chapter. The arcaded veranda, on the other hand, displays all the characteristics of post-and-beam construction as described in the first chapter: rectangular frames formed by vertical and horizontal elements with diagonal braces for consolidation and the components all assembled with mortise and tenon joints pinned with wooden dowels. The frame is left unfilled (except for the roof) to leave an open but covered outdoor space where it is pleasant to relax, socialize, or do light work in the warm season.

Figure 182. House from the Maramureş province of Romania, now in the Maramureş Ethnographic Park, Sighetul Marmatiei

Figure 183. Maramureş Ethnographic Park, Sighetul Marmatiei, Romania

Arcaded verandas are also common in the Maramureş region of northwestern Romania, and can also be found in the neighboring Carpathian region of the Ukraine. Here, though, the joinery of the braces is not done with mortise and tenons, but rather with lap (overlapping) joints. The part of the brace which is to be fitted into the post is cut into through about one half of its thickness, and the same thickness is cut out of the post which will receive the brace, following closely (but not always perfectly) its contours. (See photo of a corner post cut to receive a brace, figure 187, page 108.)

Figures 184. Maramureş Ethnographic Park, Sighetul Marmatiei, Romania

Figure 185. Arcaded porch, province of Maramureş; now in the Village Museum, Bucharest

Figures 186-188. Braces assembled with half lap joints. Maramureş Ethnographic Park, Sighetul Marmatiei, Romania

Figure 189. In the Aravis Mountains, Savoy, France

Figure 190. House from Transylvania, Romania

Figure 191. In the Aravis Mountains, Savoy, France

Figures 189-191. In some countries, a balcony may provide this covered outdoor space; they are commonly found in certain parts of Transylvania (Romania), and are typical of the chalets of the Alpine regions of France, Switzerland, and Austria. The chalet is characterized by a very long gable wall, turned toward the south wherever the terrain permits, and south-facing slopes are much sought after as building sites.

Figures 192-193. Granaries, upper Emme valley (Emmental), Switzerland. Here, as in Norway, these small houses are placed fairly close to the main farmhouse (but far enough to avoid fire spreading to it), and serve as storage houses for the family's most valued belongings.

In these constructions, the arches are simply cut out from the board structure, which encloses the veranda or balcony.

Figure 194. Balcony in an agricultural (dairy farming) village in the Emmental, Switzerland.

Figure 195. In North America, pioneer houses were usually made with a covered, but open, veranda supported by unadorned posts. This one is from the Black Creek Pioneer Village, Mississauga, Ontario, Canada.

Posts and verandas became more elaborate when the following generation(s) built more comfortable houses, often covered over with milled boards. In this early house, note the use of squared logs, dovetail corner joints, and mortar infill between the logs. Houses of this type were common also throughout the Appalachian Mountains as settlements spread through this region – formerly reserved as Indian Territory by the British colonial administration – following the independence of the United States.

Figure 196. Here, the window frame is highlighted by a wash of blue-tinted lime, as are the joints between the logs. From the Ukrainian province of Podillia; now in the Museum of Ukrainian Folk Life and Architecture, Kiev.

Figures 197-199. Decorations are often painted on the door and window frames, and also on the log ends, in the highlands of northern Slovakia.

Figures 200-205. The logs making up these houses have been squared, as described on p. 78, by taking two logs from one big tree cut in half along its length. The houses, originally built in settlements of the *Łemki* ethnic group in the Biesczady Mountains of southeastern Poland, are now in the Sanok Ethnographic Park.

Figure 206. Region of Lake Onega; now in the Kizhi Museum of Wooden Architecture, Russia

These ornate window frames, from prosperous peasants' houses in northwest Russia, are non-structural decorative elements, cut from boards and nailed onto a traditional log jamb and lintel structure. The round logs underneath have been cut back for a more flush fit against the facade; this can best be seen in figure 206. These designs became popular in the nineteenth century, as the country came into frequent contact with the city. They are inspired by neo-classical and baroque architectural elements found commonly in St. Petersburg, which was itself consciously derived from the architecture of Central Europe.

Figure 207. Latvian Open Air Museum, Riga

Figure 208. Region of Lake Onega; now in the Kizhi Museum of Wooden Architecture, Russia

Figure 209. In the Ukrainian province of Polissia, near the Polish and the Byelorussian borders, window frames are sometimes rendered with daub and whitewashed or decorated with pigmented clay washes. Museum of Ukrainian Folk Life and Architecture, Kiev

Figure 210. House from the Romanian province of Maramureş; now in the Village Museum, Bucharest.

Figures 211-212. Small openings for aeration, extending over just two logs, can be cut into the wall without using jambs, as in this agricultural building. Wallachian Ethnological Museum, Rožnov pod Radhoštem, Czeckia

Figure 213. Granary and storehouse from the Setesdal region of Norway, now in the Norsk Folkemuseum, Oslo.

Logs, Sills, and Foundations

As the sills (bottom logs) support the weight of the entire building, they should be chosen to be particularly resistant. In Carpathian Poland, for example, although the buildings are made principally of pine, oak is often used for the sills. This species, although rarer, is denser and stronger. In northwestern Russia, where oak is lacking, pine is used throughout, but the trees are cut from areas of poor, sandy soil, because on such soils the trees grow relatively slowly, and their annual growth rings are consequently much closer together than in faster-growing trees, giving the wood greater density and strength. In Norway, where pine is the only plentiful species of big, straight trees, these are cut at high altitude for the same reasons – that is, because the growth in these unfavorable conditions is slower, giving stronger wood. The sill is selected from amongst the densest logs available, and is often thicker than the logs it supports.

Figures 214-215. North Russian church, now in the Vitoslavlitsy Ethnomuseum, Novgorod, Russia.

When placed directly on the ground, the logs in contact with an often humid soil will finish by rotting. So, to remove the logs from the humid earth and enable the air to circulate around them and dry them after rainy periods, the sills are set upon big rocks at their extremities. The minimum conditions are that the four corners of the rectangular building repose on four stones, and these are chosen for their stability. But the more points of support under the sills the better, so most often, whole foundation walls are built, albeit not to any great height (see the accompanying pictures).

The foundation walls can be used to compensate for sloping terrains in hilly country, as in the Besczady Mountains in Poland or in most parts of Norway, from which the buildings on the following pages originate.

Figure 216. Farmstead from the Gudbrandsdal, Norway; now in the Maihaugen Ethnomuseum, Lillehammer.

Figure 217. House from the Valdres region of Norway; now in the Valdres Folkemuseum, Fagernes.

Figure 218. House of the Bojki ethnic group; now in the Sanok Ethnographic Park, Poland.

Figure 219. Church from the Biesczady Mountains; now in the Sanok Ethnographic Park, Poland.

Figure 220. Granary and storehouse from Hallingdal, Norway, now in the Hallingdal Museum, Nesbyen.

Figure 221. Savoy, France

In the Alps, on the other hand, the entire ground floor and sometimes even part of the first story is usually built of stone. The house is usually set back into the slope of the hill; the ground floor is consequently partly underground. The rear underground portion serves as the stable; above is the hay barn, whose entry will be at the rear ground level.

Figure 222. Loft in the Telemark region, Norway.

The Norwegian *loft* (two stories) and *bur* (one story) are a farm's granaries and storehouses for the family valuables – Sunday clothes, best linen, etc., and because they are not lived in nor (consequently) heated, it becomes even more essential that they be removed from the humidity of the ground and exposed underneath to circulating air. For this reason, a supplementary framework of sills and upright posts was designed to further elevate these small buildings, as can be seen in the following photos. This framework also has the function of creating an overhang, which serves as a barrier to climbing mice and rats by obliging them to turn completely upside down (which they cannot do) to get around it.

The joinery of the corner posts and sills is perfectly functional, but also enhances the beauty of the building, and the elements are often sculpted. Similar systems, although somewhat less ornate, are also common in Savoy (Alpine France) and in Switzerland.

Figure 223. "Loft" and "bur" (partially visible to the left) from Telemark; now in the Norsk Folkemuseum, Oslo.

Figure 224. Detail from the base post of the "loft."

Figure 225. Detail from the base post of a "bur;" now in the West Telemark Museum, Eidsborg.

Figure 226. Detail from the base post of the "bur."

Figures 227-228. Storehouse in the Berner Oberland, Switzerland.

Figures 229-230. Granaries in canton Valais/Wallis, Switzerland.

Chapter 4

The Use of Boards

Figure 231. Telemark, Norway.

Figure 232. Hypothetical reconstitution of a Viking age building, Vikingelandsbyen, Albertslund, Denmark.

Frame Infill with Logs

Thus far, I have classified wooden buildings in two categories: frame (post and beam) construction, or log construction. There are, however, buildings that show characteristics of both of these types.

If we refer back to Chapter 1, you will see how in protohistoric times, branches or small tree trunks were trimmed at their ends to fit into a groove in the vertical post framework, and were then set in horizontally. This could also be done (and was) with bigger trunks. Thus, a post-and-beam framework with an infill of logs was an often-used option, and developed, as we shall see in the following pages.

Figures 233-234. Frame construction with log infill.
Stables from Polissia province, Ukraine, now in the Museum of Ukrainian Folk Life and Architecture, Kiev.

Figure 235. Although most often, posts will be used at the corners as in the preceding examples, some buildings may have posts only at intervals in the walls, the horizontal logs being assembled at the corners with lap joints, as shown in this house from the Maramureş province of Romania, now in the Village Open Air Museum, Bucharest.

Boards

In a similar fashion, a tree trunk could be cut, or split, into still more numerous, thinner sections to become boards. The boards could, like the logs in the preceding examples, be slid into the grooves of the framework.

Whether boards or logs are used as infill for the frame structure, they can be set, as shown above, horizontally, fitted into grooves in the vertical posts, or alternatively, vertically, fitted into grooves in the sills above and below.

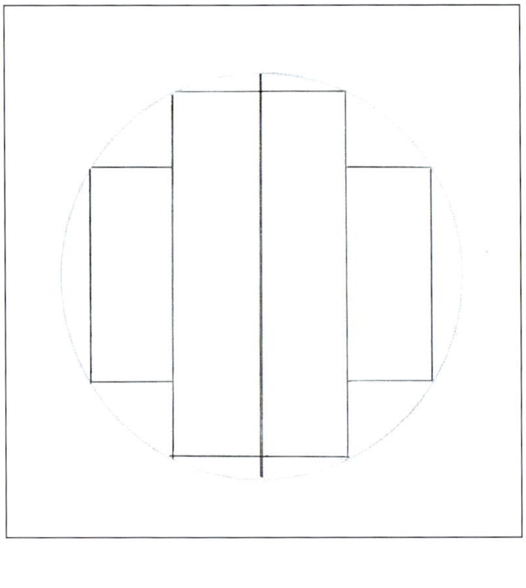

Figure 236. We can deduce, from the size of the logs used in the above photo, that several logs were taken from one very big trunk, and imagine the following theoretical cutting plan:

thickness of the squared logs: 15 or 16 cm.
diameter of the tree trunk: 80 cm.

Figures 237-238. In Upper Savoy, from Mégève to the Vallorcine, the chalets are constructed using a frame of thick posts filled with squared logs or boards.

Figure 239. Hypothetical reconstitution of a Viking home; Foteviken Viking center, Sweden.

Figures 239-241. This kind of frame construction with board or log infill was much used in Scandinavia in Viking times, and gave rise to the very impressive Norwegian "stavkyrker" of the eleventh and twelfth centuries.

Figures 240-241. Stave church from Gol, Norway; now in the Norsk Folkemuseum, Oslo.

Here the boards are set vertically and fitted into the sills (and also into the posts for those boards which juxtapose one). The boards are fairly thick, and in some churches, one side is grooved to receive the board set beside it. The other side is tapered to fit into the groove of the following board.

Figure 242. Kvitseid Bygdetun, West Telemark Museum, Norway.

In the Norwegian "loft," there is often an exterior gallery on the upper story. The gallery is enclosed by a wall of thin boards fitted into the sills. The sills, in turn, are supported by wall logs protruding from the upper part of the ground story. Often the galleries also have sculpted corner posts. In some cases, they are also built on the ground floor, as in the building shown here.

Figure 243. Telemark, Norway

Figures 244-245. Maihaugen Ethnographic Museum, Lillehammer

These enclosed galleries are sometimes also used in house architecture, as in this example, from the Gudbrandsdal, now in the Maihaugen open air museum, Lillehammer. Note the way in which the decoration has been carved out of the middle of the posts, leaving volume at the ends for assembling with the sills.

Figure 246. Loft from the Hallingdal, now in the Hallingdal Museum, Nesbyen, Norway.

Figure 247. Loft from the Hallingdal, now in the Hallingdal Museum, Nesbyen, Norway

Figures 247-248. Designs can easily be cut into boards with a 'jigsaw', a handsaw having a very thin round or multi-faceted blade with teeth facing in different directions to enable the cutter to curve or to abruptly angle the cut off in another direction. In this way, by repetition, designs can be worked into a railing, or the boards enclosing the gallery of a loft, or used to decorate the edge-boards of a roof, as is often done in Russian peasant houses.

Figure 248. Russian farmhouse from the region of Lake Onega, nineteenth century, now in the Kizhi Museum of Wood Architecture, showing decorative cutout patterns in the eaves boards and balcony railings.

Historical Evolution into the Industrial Era

Very early in time, saws existed for cutting logs into boards. These were not very common tools, as they were difficult to manufacture, attention needing to be given to the making, the beveling, and the sharpening of each tooth. The common technique for sawing, usually done by specialists equipped with the necessary tools, was to install the log at a certain height on a platform. Two men would operate a long saw, each one holding one end of the saw by a wooden handle. One would be on top of the log, the other below, on the ground. (Alternatively, a pit could be dug for the man underneath, so the log wouldn't need to be raised, or not so much.). The man above would guide the saw along a line traced beforehand, and both (but especially the man below) would provide the muscle-power. Wedges would be placed in the cut to keep it from closing up on the saw blade, and would be advanced as the cut proceeded

If a saw was not available, or if the carpenter was skilled enough and the tree sufficiently straight-grained that he felt he could gain time by splitting the log instead, he would do this in much the same way. He would open up cracks with the use of wedges pounded in with heavy hammers and advance along a line from one end of the log toward the other as the crack was opened up. The boards thus split off could then be hewed if a smooth surface was required.

Figure 249. Outdoor working space for hewing boards after they have been split off of the tree trunk. Foteviken Museum and Viking Reserve, Höllviken, Sweden

Figure 250. Ahlan's house in Haute Provence, France. Some of the posts are visible, whereas other elements of the frame are covered over with boards. The basic form is that of an irregular octagon. The roof, which is covered with flat stones in the local tradition, is also irregular, creating visual diversity, as well as providing a channel for rainwater runoff (at the far right), where it can easily be collected.

Mechanized saws powered by flowing water were often established along rivers. But it was the invention of motors able to drive saws that put milled lumber on the market at prices inferior to that which would be paid to the workmen doing the tasks manually. At the same time, or very soon thereafter, factories were established to mass-produce iron nails at prices infinitesimally lower than those at which a blacksmith could earn a living producing nails at a forge. The result of these two developments was that frame structures were subsequently mounted using lumber of small, standardized dimensions turned out by factories, nailed together with nails now cheap and plentiful, by carpenters who knew nothing of the traditional joinery techniques, which were now practically obsolete. Onto these frames could be nailed a variety of possible materials, one of which was wood, in the form of milled boards, which needed only to be cut with a saw to the proper length.

As the twentieth century advanced, transportation first by rail and then by truck enabled manufactured products – nails and milled lumber, but also alternative materials such as factory-made bricks, cement blocks, plaster-board, particle board, plywood, fiberglass insulation, and tin roofing and siding – to be transported with ever-increasing ease, until by the middle of the century, very few places remained which were inaccessible to such technological progress.

As you have been able to guess by the affection with which I have presented the traditional buildings in the preceding pages, I find them far more attractive than their modern counterparts. To be not entirely negative, though, I wish to point out the creative possibilities of the modern frame techniques, when adapted by creative people. Some of these can be seen in books like *Handmade Houses – the Wood Butchers' Art, Homework,* and more recently Lloyd Kahn's new book, *Carpenters of the Pacific Northwest.* The modern, lightweight frame can be made to twist and turn, if the time is taken to put it together that way, creating interesting nooks and crannies. Windows and skylights of many different shapes can be created, and that wonderful modern development – double-paned glass, which has a reasonable insulating capacity – allows a house to be opened visually but not physically to the nature which surrounds it. The above-mentioned books also touch on the stories of some of these builders, who often have only modest means, but make up for that in determination and inspiration.

Many contemporary builders are also turning again to the use of whole logs, big or small, without a visit to the sawmill. Some use the time-tested techniques of Russia or Scandinavia, the same ones that were adopted by many North American pioneers. Others invent new forms for roofs and stairways, drawing on almost-forgotten Amerindian techniques, like that of the Navajo hogans with their piling up of offset octagons diminishing in size, or taking their inspiration from the spirals and vortexes in nature.

After considering different roofing practices in the next chapter, we will pass on to a study of carpentry techniques of pre-industrial times; a study which may leave us more receptive to what it is possible for us to do today, be it with a new, or with a centuries-old, inspiration.

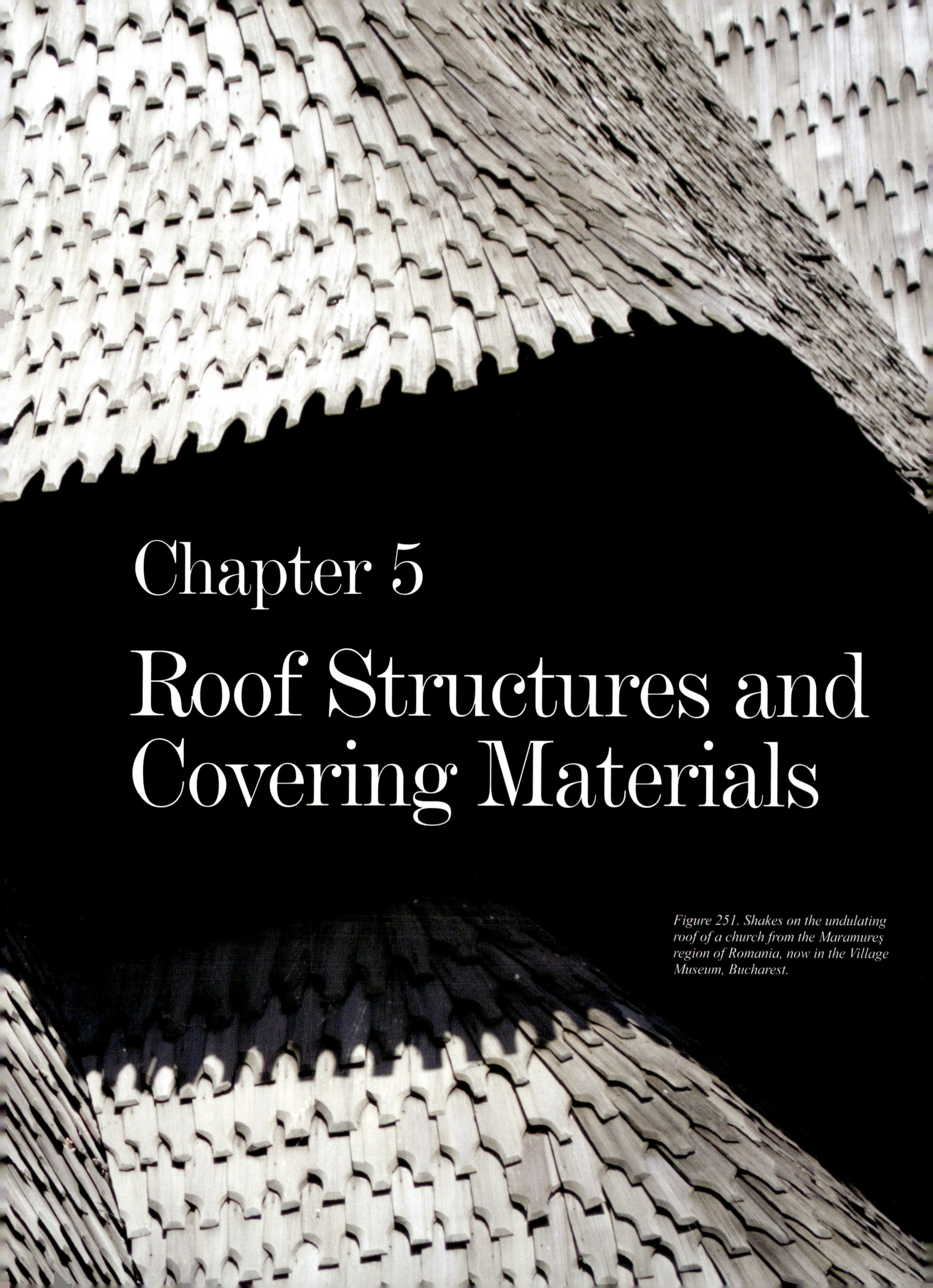

Chapter 5

Roof Structures and Covering Materials

Figure 251. Shakes on the undulating roof of a church from the Maramureş region of Romania, now in the Village Museum, Bucharest.

Roof Structures

Some definitions are necessary for understanding this subject. Please refer to the accompanying diagram:

Purlins: logs or large beams, round or squared, resting on the end walls or on *trusses* which rest on the end walls. The purlins are horizontal, and run the length of the building. They can support rafters (although some roof structures may be rafterless, as in figure 254).

Rafters: medium-size beams which rest on the purlins, or, in roof structures where purlins are not used, on the *wall plates.* In this case, they will be joined, in opposing pairs, at their top ends (as in figures 273 and 274), or will rest on a *ridge beam*, as in the diagram.

Trusses: triangular structures made up of several pieces; there are many possible combinations, of which the one illustrated in the drawing is a common one. They can be placed at the ends of the building (and also, if additional members are needed for greater strength, at intervals along its length), resting on the sidewalls.

Trusses and their reinforcing members may be multiplied and recombined according to the needs or the preferences of the carpenter. The more weight the roof must bear – by its size, or by the weight of its covering materials (flat stones or clay tiles for instance), or in snowy regions – the more the roof structure must be reinforced, and a wide variety of solutions have been imagined. This drawing shows a common roofing system, but this is by no means the only one.

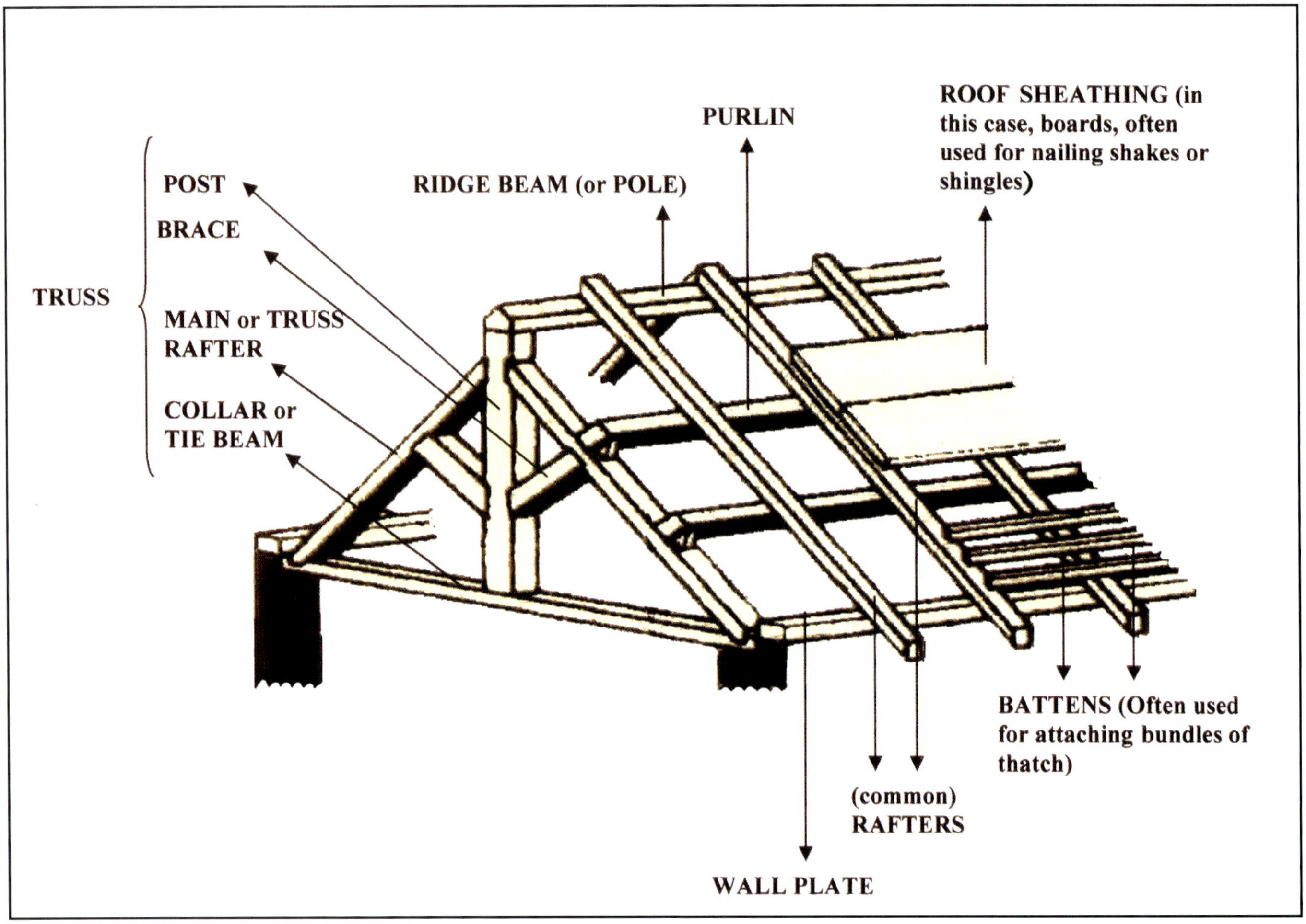

Figure 252.

Throughout the later centuries of the Middle Age (fifteenth to seventeenth), the carpenters' art developed, aided by the existence of crafts guilds, and this art served to cover stone as well as wooden buildings. From the poor peasants' hovels to the houses of prosperous farmers, from the manor houses of the country squires to the castles of counts or dukes, from the parish church to the cathedral, the demands both of the buildings and of their owners continued to grow. It is interesting to note here that even for vaulted stone churches and cathedrals, the vaults are not impermeable, and must be covered in other ways. Colossal roof structures were consequently erected on top of the buildings' walls to support a waterproof covering above the vaults.

But let us return here to the more simple types of roofs, those we see in the rural buildings depicted throughout this book.

One of the simplest roofs is a variant where there are no rafters but only roof beams upon which the roofing material is laid directly. This type of roof was common for peasant houses in Russia and in Scandinavia. The roof beams are notched into the logs forming the upper, triangular part of the gable wall, and help to hold them in place. In early times, each wall log was paired with a roof beam, and these were consequently fairly close to each other. But as this system put a lot of weight on the walls, the builders ended up by using fewer beams, setting them in only at every third or fourth level of the gable (see the following page).

Figure 253. Stable from Telemark, now in the Norsk Folkemuseum, Oslo.

Figure 254. House from the Gudbrandsdal, Norway, now in the Maihaugen Open Air Museum, Lillehammer.

Figure 255. In this house from Carelia (northwest Russia), here being re-assembled at the Kizhi Museum of Wooden Architecture, the roof beams are placed with one tied into every fourth log of the gable wall. The problem with this system, however, is that the intermediate gable logs are not securely locked into the structure (other than being pinned to the logs above and below). To compensate the instability of the gable wall triangle, then, Russian builders often built internal dividing walls into the gables, which would maintain their logs in position. If they didn't want to divide the attic space, they would instead notch in two rows of short logs, having no other function than to consolidate the gable. These can be seen from the inside in Figure 256, and from the outside on the photo in Figure 255.

Figure 256. Kizhi Museum of Wooden Architecture, Russia.

Roofing with Boards

Of this type of rafterless roof, the traditional Russian roof is a special example, characterized by the use of long, thick boards as the covering material.

A first layer of boards, set side by side and running from peak to eaves, forms a first layer of protection. But, of course, some rainwater will leak through the spaces between the boards regardless of how small these might be, so another layer of boards is placed over the first, offset in relation to it, so that the joints between the boards of the upper layer are directly (or almost) above the centers of the boards of the lower layer. Each of the upper boards is slightly concave, carved out with a curved drawknife, so that the water will run to its center. The rain that does penetrate between the boards will fall onto the middle of an underlying board. These each have two grooves (about 1 cm deep by about 2 cm wide), one close to each edge, which will collect the rainwater and make sure it is evacuated downward to flow out over the eaves.

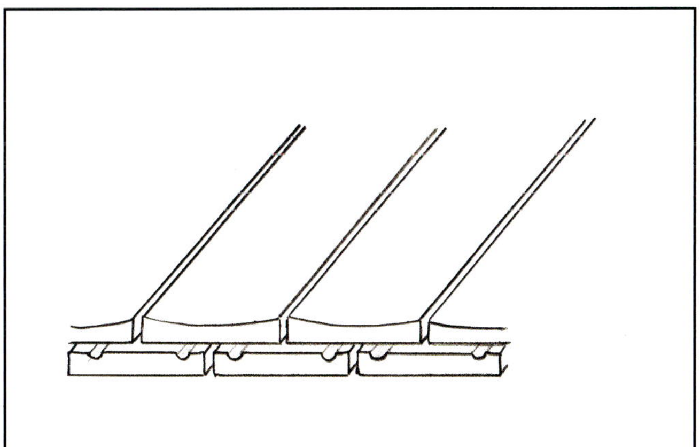

Figure 257.

Figure 258. In small buildings, like this granary from the Lake Onega region, Carelia, the boards run from the eaves to the roof ridge. Kizhi Museum of Wooden Architecture, Russia

The boards may be six meters long: for big roofs (which are characteristic of the Russian farm, where all the functions other than the bathhouse and the granaries are under the same roof), two or even three lengths of boards may be necessary, overlapping slightly; for the small buildings (bathhouse and granaries, or the more modest houses of artisans or poor peasants), a single length of boards will suffice, running from the roof ridge to the eaves.

The roof ridge and the eaves are characterized by logs hollowed to fit over the board ends and hold them in place above and below. The eaves' logs receive the two layers of boards and the water, which they shed. They are set with a slight slope to carry the rainwater off to one side of the building. Their ends are often carved for decoration.

They seem to float in the air, but on looking closely, one can see two or three (or even more, for large buildings) hooked wooden pieces holding them, disappearing beneath the roof. If we find them again on the inside of the building, we can see that they are notched into the purlins (roof beams), which they cross, and are thus held onto the building structure. These pieces are young pine trees unearthed with their roots, of which one or two will be left, cut off at about 20 cm from the trunk, to form a bracket in which the eaves log is lodged. The ensemble is a well-conceived balancing feat, which has been used now for many centuries.

Figure 259. Church, Kizhi Museum of Wooden Architecture.

Figure 260. House, Kizhi Museum of Wooden Architecture.

Figure 261. Granary from the Lake Onega area, Russia. Now in the Kizhi Museum of Wooden Architecture.

Figure 262. House, Kizhi Museum of Wooden Architecture.

This type of roof was to be found in former times all over western Russia, from Arkhangelsk through Lake Onega to Novgorod, and on into the Ukraine. A similar one several centuries old, which can be seen in the open-air Museum of Pereieslav-Khmelnitsky in the Ukraine, demonstrates the link between the traditions of the original land of the "Rus" and that of northern Russia.

Figure 263. House, Vitoslavlitsy Ethnographic Park, Novgorod, Russia.

At the roof ridge, another log (or series of logs, for long buildings) covers the joint where the boards from each side meet. The log is hollowed out in an inverted V to fit over the roof's ridge, and its weight helps maintain the boards in place. The ends of the ridge log are usually hewed or sculpted to resemble (often in stylized fashion) the head of a horse, an old pagan symbol of the sun's diurnal crossing of the sky. Moreover, a solar wheel is also a common decorative element, and is often carved into boards places along the roof's edges or hanging from the summit of the roof at either or both of its extremities.

Figure 264. Granary, Kizhi Museum of Wooden Architecture.

Figures 268-269. House from the sixteenth century, now in the Ethnographic Park of Pereieslav-Khmelnitsky, Ukraine.

Figure 270. Stable from the Telemark region, now in the Norsk Folkemuseum, Oslo, Norway.

Living Roofs

In Norway, the ancient tradition of the "living roof" is still frequently seen, a tradition that also existed in Sweden and in Finland, but which has been less maintained in those two countries.

Here, the roof beams are covered with boards, which serve as a support, and birch bark, which will not rot or mildew in contact with humidity. The bark is stripped from the living tree in sheets, which will prevent the rainwater from penetrating through the roof when they are properly overlapped. On top of this layer are placed clumps of earth containing grass, which will continue to grow, its roots finishing by linking the earth into a cohesive mass. Part of the rainwater falling onto the roof will be absorbed by this mass; the rest will run off over the birch bark layer.

Figure 271. Telemark, Norway

Figure 272. Stable/barn in two parts with a common roof to allow wagons and workers to be sheltered in the passageway. From the Østerdal region of Norway; now in the Norsk Folkemuseum, Oslo.

Figure 273. This roof being uncovered for restoration, we can see its structure of rafters consolidated with tie beams. L'vov Ethnographic Park, Ukraine.

Other Simple Roof Structures

Another simple system uses rafters but without roof beams. The rafters, which must be fairly light if they are not to need supporting beams, are blocked at their base by being notched into a sill set on top of the wall. They are assembled in pairs, one springing from each side of the house, and are joined at their top ends by a lap joint. The pairs of rafters are maintained in place by other elements (boards or battens) attached perpendicular to them and running the length of the building. These elements will also serve as a support for the covering material. In Neolithic period constructions, these elements were lashed together with cords made of fibers; later in time they were fixed with tree nails (wooden dowels), and since the industrial era, with steel or iron nails.

This rudimentary roof structure is just the bare minimum, and can generally carry only a light weight, such as a thatch roof. One simple way of consolidating such a structure is to add a "tie-beam" to each pair of rafters; this will prevent the rafters from being pushed apart at their base.

Figures 274-276. Consolidating the rafters with a "tie beam," showing different types of joinery:

1) A partial lap joint, held in place with a dowel
Latvian Open Air Museum, Riga

2) Lap joint with dowel, reinforced by a leather lashing (which seems superfluous to me)
Lejre Archeological Research center, Denmark

3) Recessed partial dovetail joint
Foteviken Viking Reserve, Sweden

Figure 277. Sanok Ethnographic Park, Poland

Figure 278. Sanok Ethnographic Park, Poland

Thatched Roofs

When making a thatch roof, the bundles of straw (or reeds, or another suitable material) are lashed to battens resting on the rafters. The first bundles to be placed are attached at the bottom of the roof, to form the eaves, and the construction continues toward the ridge with each layer placed overlapping the one beneath.

The bundles can be nearly aligned at their bottom ends to give a layered effect, or the straw can be bundled irregularly for a more homogeneous aspect.

Figures 279-281. Riga Ethnographic Park, Latvia

Shake Roofs

Wooden shakes, or shingles, which, like thatch, have been used as a roofing material for thousands of years (see Chapter 1), can be trimmed in many different ways for decorative effects. They can, as well, be tongue and grooved on one side to fit together tightly with no permeable joint, or overlapped systematically on one side (or on one side and then on the other, in alternative courses), or simply laid flat, each course overlapping the preceding one by more than half its length to ensure the proper runoff of rainwater (see the schema on this page).

Figure 283. The Village Museum, Bucharest, Romania

Shakes are traditionally made by splitting up segments of a log 35 to 70 cm long (1 to 2 feet). This can be done with a thin hatchet, as in this photo taken at the Village Museum, Bucharest, Romania, or with a "froe," a blade attached perpendicular to a handle. In any case, the cutting edge of the tool, which is used, is first placed where desired, and then struck with a mallet. Since the pieces split radially off the trunk will be thicker on the outside than on the inside, it is possible to cut a groove into the thicker side.

One can also shape the ends to the form one wishes with a drawknife (see photo).

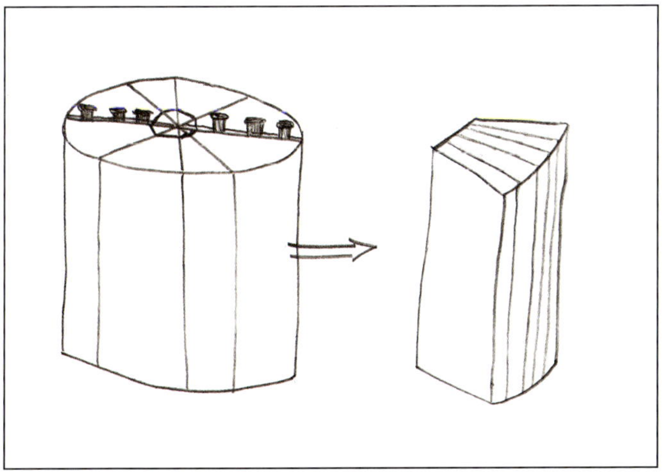

Figure 282. The block is split up, ideally into eight approximately equal sections, with wedges of iron or hard wood. The heart (inside) wood, too soft to be durable, is removed, and the pieces are further split up with a froe or a hatchet.

Figure 284. The Village Museum, Bucharest, Romania

Figure 285. Shake roof covering a small church in the Bieszczady Mountains of Poland; now in the Sanok Open Air Museum. Another photo of the same church, viewed from the rear, can be seen on page 118. The charm of this building comes, to a great extent, from the overhanging roof, which gives the impression of a gnome's bonnet, placed on wall logs which protrude well beyond the corners, and whose extremities are irregularly cut.

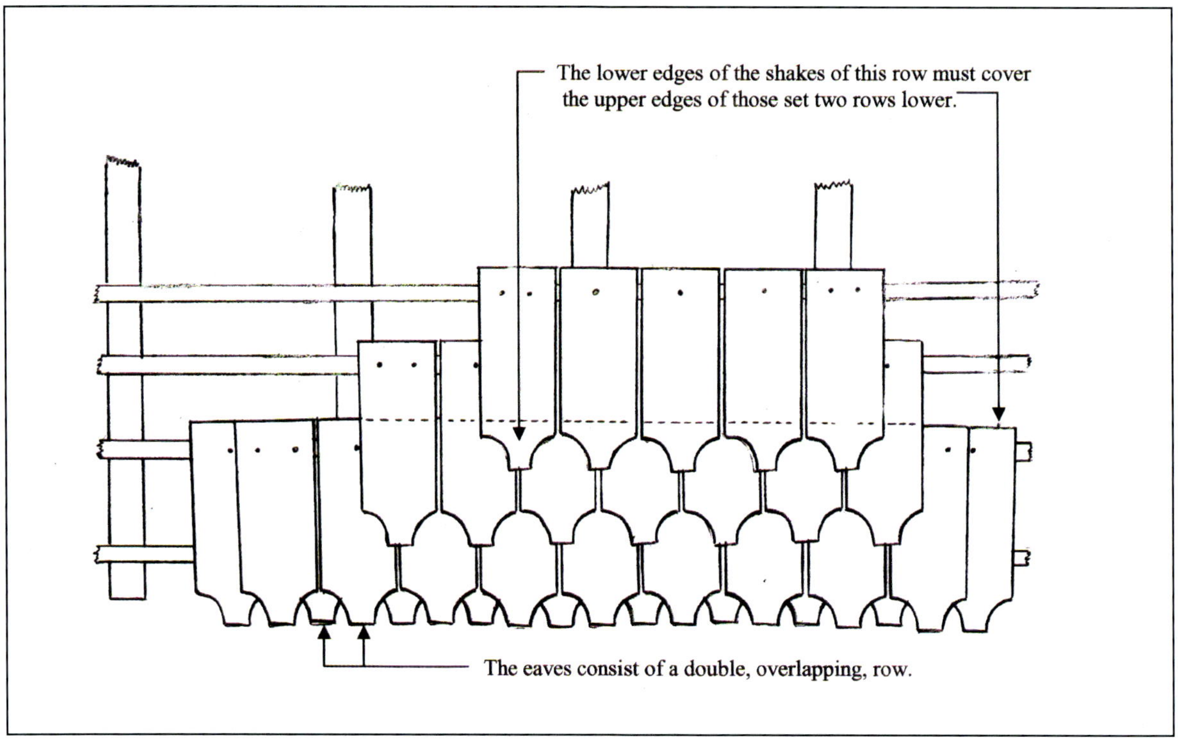

Figure 286.

Figure 287. Tens of thousands of aspen shakes, dressed by axe to give them their curving form, cover the Church of the Transfiguration (UNESCO World Heritage Site), with its twenty-three domes, on the island of Kizhi. Kizhi Museum of Wooden Architecture, Russia.

Chapter 6

The Carpenter's Handbook

Carpentry Techniques from Yesteryear

Figure 288.

A General Approach to Working Wood with Hand Tools

The fibrous structure (the grain) of a tree is an important factor in determining whether the wood is easy or difficult to work. The regularity of this structure differs from one species to another. Aleppo pine, for instance, commonly found in Provence and visibly twisty, has an irregular, fibrous structure not easy to work, whereas the straight pines of the Cévennes (or the Jura, or the Vosges) have a straighter grain, making them easier to split and work with hand tools. In North America, we could similarly compare the twisty Ponderosa pine with the straight Douglas fir, much preferred, where available, for log building.

Experience will soon reveal to you the problems of adapting to the wood's fibrous structure – but for those who haven't yet acquired this experience, I will say a few words about this now in the hopes of shortening your learning time:

Figure 289. When you see that the axe (or whatever cutting tool you may use) isn't cutting the wood and leaving it smooth, but rather, is tearing into it (as in this photo, for the part above the knot), you should work in the opposite direction.

Figure 290. Around a knot, the fibers turn and may radically change direction. This is the case in Figure 289, where the work was done from the bottom toward the top, with the result you see. You can anticipate this and work the other side in the opposite direction, which I have done in Figure 290 and which has pretty much corrected the problem. But knots are always tricky.

Figure 291. The fibers may run across a line to which you wish to hew. When this happens, work in the other direction so that you don't tear into the part that you wish to keep intact. The first step in hewing a surface is to make a series of scoring cuts (already removed in this photo, but visible in Figure 292). This makes hewing off the excess wood much easier by breaking up the mass to be removed, and also guards against your axe strokes going too far if they happen to open up the wood along a line of fibers running in an unfavorable direction. You will find a detailed description of this practice on p. 185.

Figures 292-293. Here, the finish work must be done from left to right to avoid tearing into your line. (See the way the fibers are running, clearly visible in Figure 292.) If you are right-handed, then, you will stand on the other side of the log to achieve the finish shown in Figure 293.

Figure 294. Because the trunk is round, the axe will meet the fibers at a different direction from one side to the other on the same surface, and will thus cut through them on one side, but will rip them on the other. By anticipating this, you can work each side in the direction most suitable for each.

The Round or "Saddle" Notch

Figure 294a.

The Round or "Saddle" Notch

Figure 294b.

N.B. For this demonstration, we have systematically cut the notch in the bottom part of each log, whereas in the sketches on pages 66 and 68, Chapter 3, it is shown cut into the top of each log.

Either system can be used, but whichever you choose, you must use it consistently.

Making a saddle notch can be done in three steps:

i) trace and cut the notch;
ii) trace and cut the groove in the bottom of the log
iii) adjust your cuts for a precise fit.

Figure 295. The next log to be used in the wall is put in position on top of the logs that are to receive it. A position can be found, perhaps by rolling the log a little, in which it will be fairly stable (If not, fix it in place with a "log dog" as shown.)

Trace a vertical axis on the end of the log using a plumb bob. Align this axis with those that have already been traced on the logs below.

Figure 296. If the log is stable enough, you can begin marking it; if not, it can be held in place with a pair of "log dogs."

Figure 297. With some kind of tracing tool (in the case shown here, a compass with two metal points), open the points to correspond to the distance between the logs.

Figures 298-299. Keeping the two compass points vertically aligned when viewed both from in front and from the side, draw the tool along the logs with the bottom point touching the rounded contour of the lower log and leaving a mark on the upper one. This process is called scribing. Repeat the scribing on the opposite side of the log, and also on the two sides of its other end (i.e., at the other corner). This means making four scribing marks.

This operation takes some practice to master. Some potential difficulties are:

—Keeping the two compass points vertically aligned from both in front and from a side view. You must move your head to change your angle of vision while scribing, without letting your hands deviate. There exist modern scribing tools with bubble levels incorporated for easier verification, but they are not common. In any case, you will soon learn to coordinate the eye and the hand.

—The compass points may jump or snag on irregularities of the log. Ideally, your scribing tool will have points (not too sharp) which curve slightly outward to pass more easily along the log's surface while still maintaining contact.

Figure 300. 3. Turn the log over. Go over the scratched lines with a pencil to make them more visible and to complete any missed parts (especially on the underside, which was difficult to get at with the compass points during scribing). Your four scribing marks will then be joined to make the outlines of two notches, one at each end.

Figure 301. In the absence of anything better, you can always make a compass by inserting a wooden wedge in between two pencils and taping them together. But this will not last long, and is only a stop-gap solution

Figures 302-303. 4. Start chopping. You can go at it with heavy strokes in the center, in a V-shape, with your hands well apart and toward the bottom of the handle. As you approach the limits of your tracings, ease up on the force of your blows, proceeding more carefully with hands closer together and higher up on the handle for more control.

Figures 304-305. Following the lines is easy at first, but as they curve more and more toward the bottom of the notch, you will have more and more difficulty getting in with your cutting edge held at the proper cutting angle. At this point, you can use just the bottom half of the cutting edge, making a series of small cuts close together and just deep enough to barely touch the line.

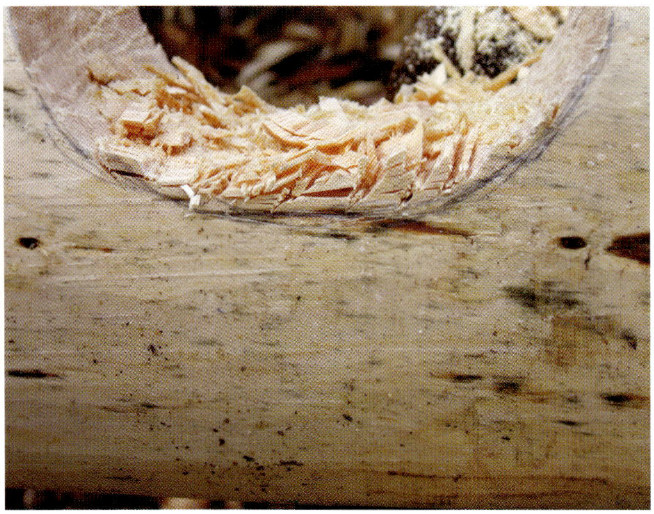

Figures 306-307. You can then use the cutting edge of the axe, holding the axe head directly in your hands, to cut out the pieces left loosely attached to the line.

Figure 308. Similarly, when your notch has been well gouged out and you're within a few millimeters of the bottom, you can get right down to your line (which, in the middle, you have to judge by eye) by making a series of shallow cuts in a cross-hatched pattern.

You can then scrape off these loosened-up pieces using the axe head held in your two hands. It will be impossible to get a smooth finish without using other tools, but you needn't; with the axe alone, you can get to within 1 mm of perfection.

6. Do the same thing at the log's other end to hew out the other notch. Then turn the log over and set it in place.

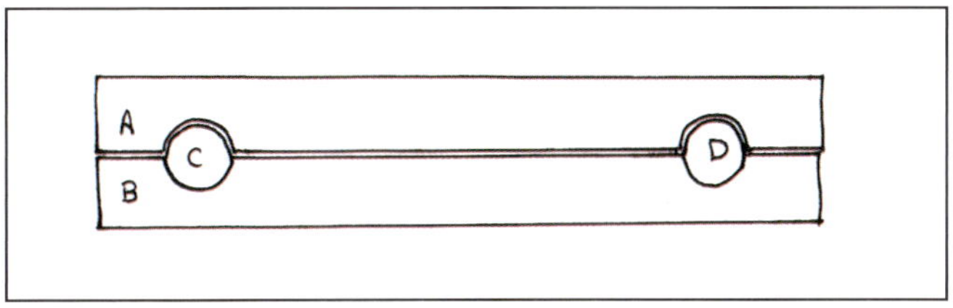

Figure 309. In theory, if your tracing and cutting was correct, you will now have this (at RIGHT): logs A and B will be touching all along their length, and the notches will just fit over the perpendicular logs C and D.

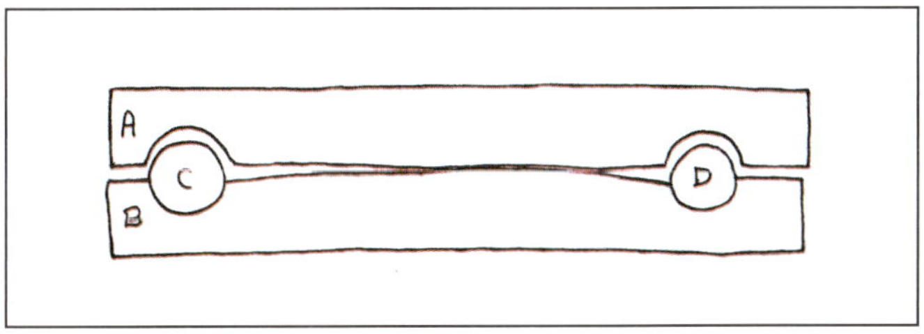

Figures 310-311. But just a bump (or several) in one of the logs will keep A from sitting snugly against B, and the notches will be well above the curves of C and D. But don't worry; you will take care of that with the next step.

Figures 312-313. With the log in position, determine the depth of the groove to be cut in its underside so that it will settle well down onto the curve of the log below. This distance must be at least as much as that separating the two logs under the notches. Take this distance, or a bit more as you see fit, as your compass opening, and scribe it on the log's end, as shown; when you do this, you can judge if the overlap is sufficient.

Figure 314. Next, scribe a line along the entire length of the log, on both of its sides.

Figure 315. Then turn the log over and go over the scratched lines with a pencil to make them easily visible; you will then have the contours of the groove to be cut. These will be as regular, or irregular, as are the logs to be assembled.

Figures 316-317. Cut out the groove between the lines. Here, it is better to cut too deeply than not enough; if you don't cut out enough, the logs will touch somewhere along their length and not allow a good fit; you will then have to locate the offending places and retouch them. If, on the other hand, you cut too deeply, the extra space created will simply be filled and closed by the fiber insulation when this is put in.
To cut the groove, first lightly score the surface (figure 316); then chop lightly from the outside of the groove toward its inside to hollow it out.

Figures 318-319. After cutting the groove, put the log in place and appraise the fit. A few adjustments and this should be perfected with only a few mm of error here and there, which will be filled with the insulation. And as you gain experience, you will be able to do this with increasing speed and accuracy.

Figures 320-321. CERTAIN REFINEMENTS HAVE BEEN DEVELOPED to minimize any play and consequent deformation at the corners. The notch can be cut with a bar of wood left in its interior; a corresponding groove will then be cut into the log with which it is meant to be assembled. If this is done, the notches must be cut with a chisel or a gouge rather than with an axe, and a lot more time is spent in its execution.

More complex still is the joinery system seen in this photo (lower right), part of a pedagogic display at the Kizhi Museum of Wooden Architecture, Russia.

Squaring a Log

Figure 321a.

TRACING THE OUTLINE

Figure 322. [1.] At one end of the log, trace a vertical central axis using a plumb bob on a thin cord. (This may go through the center of the tree's growth rings, but this is not necessarily the center of the log's volume; let an attentive and discerning eye be your guide.)

Then, on either side of this axis, trace two more lines, measuring with a ruler to get them rigorously parallel to and equidistant from it. These two lines will be your "side" lines; they will correspond to the sides of the log once it has been squared. You choose the width you want (optimally, between 15 and 18 cm for reasonable insulation). ALL your logs must be squared to the same width, whatever you may choose (except for internal partition walls, which may be thinner).

Then trace the other end of the log in the same way.

Figure 323. [2.] In principle, your axis lines at each end of the log will be parallel (and consequently, your side lines also). It is advisable, though, at least until you are sure of the accuracy of your tracings, to verify them. To do this, have a buddy hold a long straight board with one edge along one of the lines you have drawn. (If you are alone, you can prop it up, or nail it lightly in place.)

Figure 325. [4.] You will then have something like this on both ends of the log.

Figure 324. [3.] Then go to the other end of the log and apply another straight-edged board against that end. You must then line up (by eye) the edges of the two boards to be parallel, as shown in the accompanying photo.

AN ALTERNATIVE METHOD FOR MARKING OFF THE OUTLINE

Figure 326. [1.] On one end of the log, trace a central axis approximately vertical (by eye; don't bother with a plumb bob). Then, mark off a parallel line on either side, measuring to be sure that the lines are rigorously parallel to, and equidistant from, the axis.

Figure 327. [2.] Have someone hold (or if you're alone, nail lightly in place) a straight-edged board aligned along the axis, then go to the other end of the log.

Figure 328. [3.] On the other end, apply another straight-edged board through the log's center (as judged by eye). You must then align this straight edge with the one on the log's other end so that they are perfectly parallel. (This is also indicated in the preceding method; but whereas there this step was optional, merely as a verification, here it is obligatory, because the initial axis was not drawn with the plumb bob.) Using the edge of the board, trace a line that will be your central axis. It will necessarily be parallel to the axis first drawn on the other end.

Figure 329. [4.] Mark off your two side lines (as in step 1.) on either side of the axis. Both of the log's ends will then be marked as shown.

Figure 330. [5.] Take a snap-line (a cord which can be stretched taut) covered with chalk (blue leaves a good visible line), and stretch it from one edge line to the opposite one along the length of the log. This is best done by two people, but if you are alone, you can tie one end of the string to a small-diameter nail that you drive precisely into the point where the edge line meets the circumference of the log.

Snap the line, as in the photo, to mark your new "hewing line."

Figure 331. [6.] Do this again on the other side, then turn the log over and do it again on both sides of its bottom. You will then have four chalk lines, which, taken in pairs, show you the side limits of your log to be hewed square. You will hew along the edge lines drawn on each end of the log, to the limit of the chalk lines, top and bottom, on each side. (Many experienced carpenters do not bother tracing the lines along the bottom of the log, but just hew straight down, by eye, from the top lines. This does shorten the time taken, as long as your hand / eye coordination is good.)

Figure 332. The log is then turned through a 1/4 rotation to have the part that will be hewed facing upward. It is then "scored" as shown. The tools that can be used for this work will be described and discussed below.

The scoring marks are spaced at intervals of 10-25 cm. (You choose—the closer you space them, the less effort you will have to make in the next step, hewing off the intervening wood.)

Figure 333. The scoring marks should go to almost exactly the depth of the wood to be hewed off. That is, they should make a straight line at the bottom of the grooves between the two blue chalk lines.

Figure 334. Once the scoring has been done, the log is then turned again through a 1/4 rotation so that the scoring is to the side. This side of the log will then be "hewed to the line" – that is, to the chalk lines – along its entire length.

Hewing

Figures 335-337. The carpenter hews to the line.

Figures 338-339. As he approaches the line, the cuts become wafer thin.

Figure 340. Once one side has been hewed, the log will then be turned over, and the opposite side scored, then hewed to the line.

Figure 343. When tracing the top and bottom lines, you can get a maximum amount of material out of the log by establishing these lines as far apart as possible. Unlike the width, which must be constant throughout (refer back to step 1), the height can vary from log to log, and also from one end of the log to the other. You must simply alternate big ends and small ends as you build your wall upwards, to keep the logs more or less horizontal.

Figure 341. Then, the top (or the bottom) is traced, scored, and hewed as before.

Figure 342. This is the finished log, which has just a very small amount of "flash" (a portion of the curved circumference of the log remaining where the dressed surfaces do not quite meet).

Variations in the Method and in the Tools Used for Squaring

When I was a young, aspiring builder, I read with enthusiasm an article about how Appalachian settlers squared the logs for their homes and farm buildings. The article presented *the* method as if it were invariable and inviolable. It said that scoring was done with a felling ax, and hewing with a broadax. Well, that set me back a lot, because it took me a long time to find a broadax. When I finally did find one, it was very big and heavy, and I found it quite unwieldy, and was quickly discouraged. I even dropped carpentry work (for a time) to try my hand at working with stone, where I found I had more success.

Figure 344. For this demonstration, we preferred using the felling axe for taking off the big pieces between the scoring marks; the broadax (foreground) was used for the hewing and also for the scoring.

When I finally did come back to wood, and went traveling and observing through eastern Europe, I saw that Russian carpenters used the same axe, a simple felling axe, for almost all their work (except where personal preference determined otherwise); they scored and hewed their logs with one and the same ax. Just a simple axe, an axe sold in most tool stores. No one-sided bevel, no worry about right-handed or left-handed use. And it worked just fine (see the following photos of Russian carpenters at work), as it has for centuries. When I got back home, I was able to simply go to an ordinary hardware store, buy an ordinary ax, sharpen it well, and set to work. Successfully.

There are a variety of tools traditionally used for squaring logs, or for doing any operation. The favorite tool depends a lot on where you are, and what your daddy or the people around you use, and what you've gotten used to. I have found that if I got used to a certain type of tool, that it felt good to me, and if I tried something different, it usually didn't feel as good. But if my favorite tool was lost and couldn't be replaced, and I had to persist with the other one, it got to feeling all right, too. I might not even have realized how right it felt had I not had the opportunity one day to once again work with a tool like my first one, only to find that it felt unwieldy, and I preferred the one I had gotten used to recently. The moral of the story, in simple folk terms is: make do with what you got.

It is important, though, to keep your axes, and other cutting tools, well sharpened. You should be able to sharpen a pencil with them.

For the preceding demonstration of log squaring, done at the Sanok Ethnomuseum in Poland by Piotr Popiel, carpenter on the museum's permanent maintenance team, and myself. Piotr and I both tried different axes for the different operations. We both preferred the broadax (traditionally used for hewing) for the scoring as well. But, at times, we both preferred the felling ax for knocking off the big pieces between the scoring lines, returning to the broadax for hewing.

Notice that Piotr's stance (with both feet on the side of the log on which he is working) is different from that of the Russian carpenters I observed, who straddle the log, as can be seen in the following photos:

Figures 345-346. Carpenter Liousha working at Kizhi Ethnomuseum, in northern Russia. He does the scoring with his habitual axe, and hews with the same.

Figure 347. Carpenter Nikolai working at Kizhi Ethnomuseum, Russia. The scoring was done with a chain saw (the use of which will be discussed later), and the hewing with the habitual Russian carpenters' axe.

Figure 348. Bo Jørgen Nielsen, specialist in Viking ship restoration, hews an oak log set up at just above knee level with a Viking era hewing axe.

Figure 349. Viking era hewing ax showing the curved handle which permits the carpenter to work at the same level as the log (or board, as in this case) while keeping his hands at a safe distance from it.

You must take care for your legs. The more your ax-strokes are vertical, the less you risk your legs – but the more you increase the chances of hewing inside your line with a misplaced stroke. Going along the log with strokes more or less diagonal to the vertical plane enables you to hew more accurately to the line. If you feel uncomfortable about this, choke up on the handle (notice how Nikolai and Liousha are holding theirs in the previous images), and swing more gently. It is also possible to keep to one side of the log instead of straddling it, and work on the side opposite, as does Piotr in the preceding demonsration, tilting it somewhat toward you. Or, with boards or logs that are light enough to be manipulated, you may prefer to raise them higher – to thigh or waist level – and hew with a medium-weight ax fitted to a shorter handle. In either of these cases, your legs are safe, and in the latter, you're not working with your back bent.

Carpentry specialists in most areas had specialized axes for hewing, but the peasant was likely to have only one, multi-purpose axe such as the Russian axes seen on page 189. In Viking times, the axe shown here was in general use, and was used for hewing, scoring, felling, chopping, and also for battle.

The specialized hewing axes can have many shapes, depending on the traditions of each territory, but the common features were their large surface area and the fact that they were beveled on one side only, presenting a large and perfectly flat surface on the other side. The flat side is the one used for hewing to the line, so that when using it, you must position yourself appropriately to the log. Most beveled axes have the bevel to the right (flat side to the left), and are used with a handle curving to the right or backwards (away from the log). This enables you to work with your hands at the same level as the log, if it is at waist level, for example, without scraping your knuckles.

But again, don't get hung up on trying to find rare tools; in the absence of such a handle, unless you want to make one yourself, work with your hands higher than the log.

OR

You can turn the surface to be dressed to face upward, as in the next method:

Figure 350. All-purpose axe of a style dating from the Viking period; Denmark.

Figure 351. Hewing axe of a style dating from the Viking period; Denmark.

Figure 352. Hewing axe; Ukraine.

Figure 353. "Goosewing" hewing axe; Ukraine.

Figures 354-357. All photos in these figures (354-357) were taken in Vikingelandsbyen, Denmark, where examples of the Viking habitat (longhouse and outbuildings) have been reconstituted using the tools and techniques of the period, or in the Museum of Folk Life and Architecture of the Ukraine, Kiev.

Figure 358. The first scoring passage.

Since I don't like working while bent over, and as I don't have an axe with a curved handle, I experimented with other ways of doing the job, and found one that, while not being quite orthodox, seemed pretty good for cases like mine. It involves turning the surface to be dressed upwards; I was subsequently working on a surface that was horizontal, at hip or waist level (which is my habit as a stonecutter).

I took a lot of liberties with the preceding indications: for the scoring, for instance, instead of cutting right to the level of the guidelines, I just quickly made a series of cuts 4 to 10 cm. deep all in the same direction while moving along the length of the log. I followed this with another passage in the opposite direction to trim off the scored part. I like the feel of doing it this way: it is quick, I am in motion, and I can swing the axe quite freely and work off energy without having to concentrate on precision (which comes nonetheless at a later stage).

Figure 359. Rough-hewing after the first passage.

Figure 360. Second scoring passage.

This first stage leaves me with a certain thickness still to be removed, as the scoring cuts are not deep. So, I would pass another time — in fact, three or more times — one time to score then hew to the line on one side, then one time to score then hew to the line on the other side, and then one more time to score and hew the part left in the middle between the two preceding hewing passes. (And each of these passages may need further work).

Nonetheless, I find the whole operation hardly longer than the methods I tried in Russia and in Poland (the same as were used by the Appalachian pioneers), and to my mind, it is more enjoyable.

Once you have gotten down to the desired level, you can finish the surface with the axe head held in both hands, pushing it obliquely, which will shave off any roughness. (You will especially want to do this with any parts that are to be in contact with the hands, or other parts of the body). If you want it smoother than this (see photo), you must work longer with the axe blade, or use a plane.

Figure 361. Rough-hewing after the second passage.

Figure 362. The finish work.

Figure 363. The finished surface.

The Chamfer

Figure 363a.

All the steps necessary for cutting a chamfer can be seen in this one photo:

1) Trace the edges of the chamfer.
2) Lightly score the surface to be removed, with an axe or a hatchet. The smaller the chamfer is, the lighter your scoring cuts must be.
3) Hew off the excess volume, as has been done to the left: if need be, pass once again to hew precisely to the two lines.

This procedure is pretty much the same as that described above for squaring one side of a log, only in miniature.

Figure 364. Roof ridge beam crafted by the author for the restoration of a roof at the Kizhi Museum of Wooden Architecture, Russia. (See "Roofs," pp. 151-155).

Overlapping (Lap) Joints

Overlapping (Lap) Joints

These can be cut halfway through one of the two pieces to be joined (we will call this a half lap joint) or one quarter of the way through each of the two pieces to be joined (which we will call the quarter lap joint). Other systems can also be improvised to catch up differences in height as the logs are piled up, according to the situation. Such joinery, used with squared logs, was originally very simple and was in use even before the Bronze Age: the advances in metallurgy did not basically change the tools with which the builders worked, but only provided sharper, longer-lasting cutting edges, allowing for greater precision in execution. But during the eighteenth century, the originally simple lap joint evolved, in some places, toward greater complexity by the cutting of interlocking parts in the interior of the joint (which are, then, invisible from the outside).

Here, we will study in detail the method of preparing the simple versions, already satisfactory for most situations, and then look briefly at some of the possible complexities that can improve the stability of the building even more. (The same evolution can be found for the notches used with round logs; see figure 320).

Here is a schema of the half lap joint (see also figure 321). The quarter lap joint (see also p. 179) seems to me even more resistant, while still remaining simple in its execution (unlike those involving interlocking parts on the inside of the joints). The accompanying illustration shows how the logs are assembled.

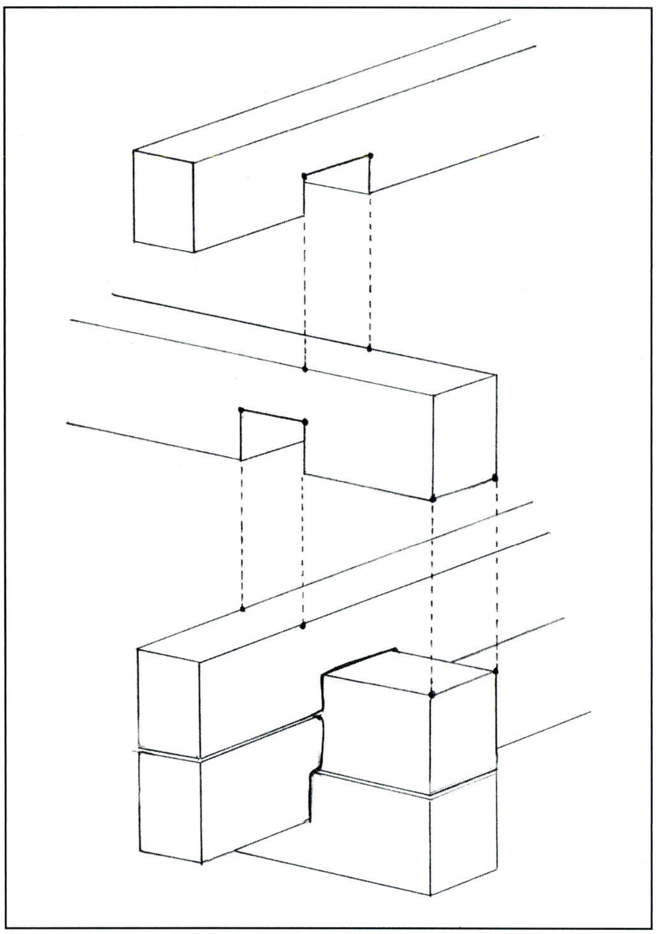

Figure 365. The half lap joint (see also page 68).

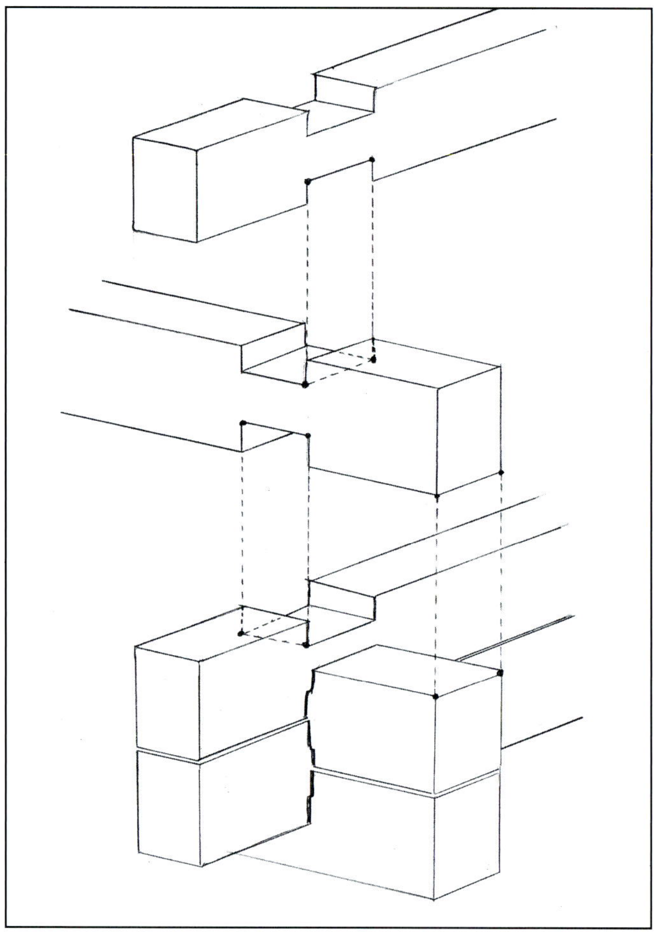

Figure 366. The quarter lap joint.

Figure 367. A notch is made in both the top and the underside of each log. The notch will be of a depth equivalent to about 1/4 the vertical height of the log, but in the case where the logs are of different thicknesses, this calculation is only approximate.

Figure 368. To determine it precisely, you must set up the next log to rest on the perpendicular log which is going to receive it, and then measure the distance which separates it from the parallel log beneath, upon which it will finish by sitting.

Figure 369. Let us say that this distance is "X". You will then divide "X" between the depths of the notches cut into C and into B. Normally, the division would be equal, but if one of the logs is much thicker than the other, you can cut more out of the thicker log, and less out of the thinner, so as not to leave it too fragile. (The same principle applies to the execution of the dovetail joint).

Measure "X"

Mark out the notches in D and E to the depth X/2
If D and E are of very different heights, however, you can divide X unequally between them so as to cut a shallower notch in the smaller one, compensating with a deeper notch in the thicker one.

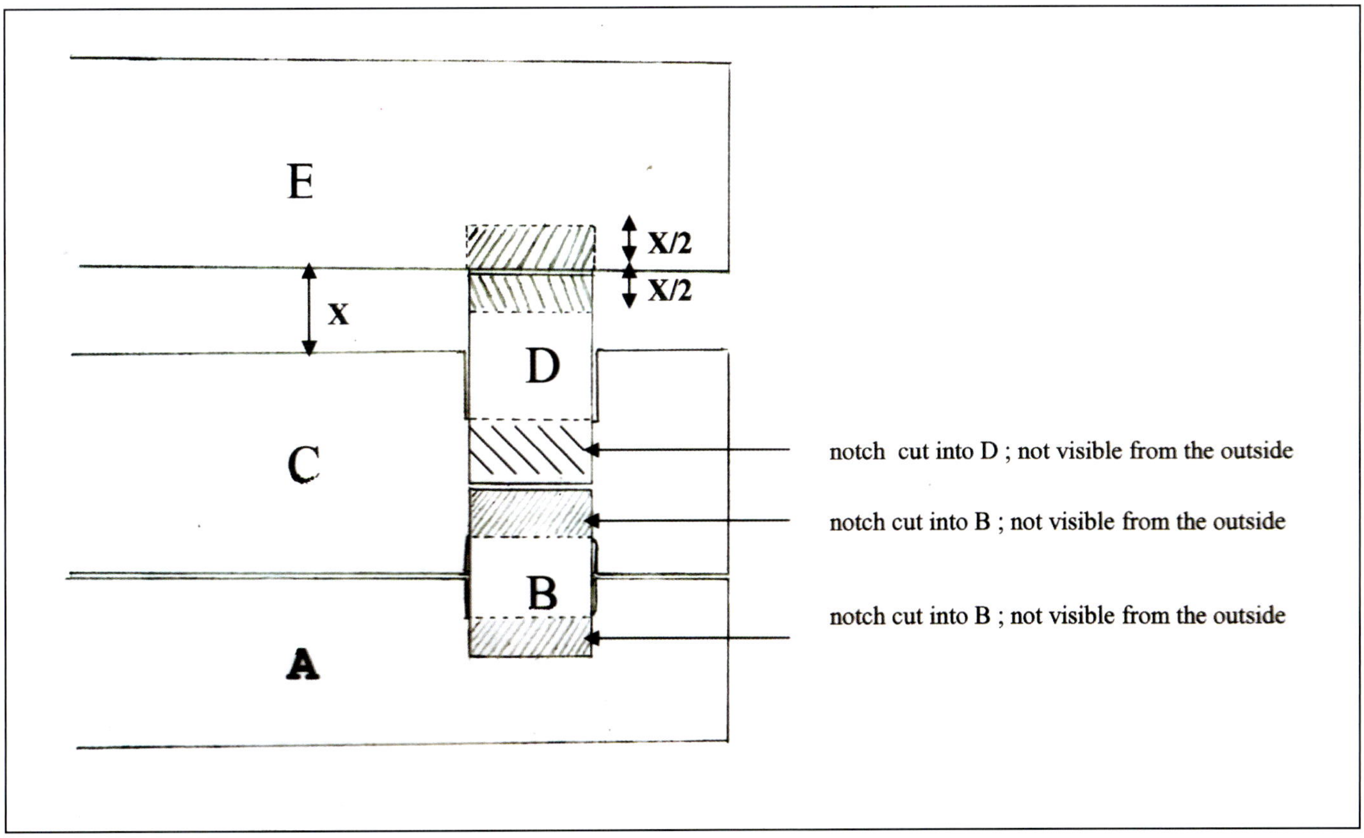

Figure 370. Start by cutting the limits of your notch with two vertical cuts (along the lines you have measured and marked on the log). You can also make one or two supplementary cuts: breaking up the mass to be taken off makes cutting it out easier.

Figure 371. You can then cut out the notch with a chisel, working between the two vertical cuts in the direction of the length of the log.

Figure 372. As you dig deeper into the wood with the chisel, you will end up by butting up against one the vertical cuts that marks the limit of the notch.

Figure 372. When you have well dug out this end, then change direction to do the same at the other. Since you are going increasingly deeper toward each end of the notch, you will inevitably leave a ridge of wood in the center, and this you will have to take off by working obliquely from the sides of the notch toward the center.

Figure 373. Level off your cut at the desired depth.

Figure 374. Verify with a ruler or other straight edge that it is indeed flat.

More Complex Joinery

Normally, in constructions where the logs meet at the angles and protrude a further 20 or 30 cm, this protruding wood acts to block the movement of the individual logs. Nonetheless, to achieve even greater resistance to movement, it is possible to make an interlocking joint within the joint by cutting a bar (or "tongue") into one piece and a corresponding groove in the other.

Figure 375. The photo shows an even more complex interlocking system, which was often used in the Zakopane area (southern Poland) since the beginning of the eighteenth century. In this photo, the upper log has been turned a quarter of a turn so that you can see how it is notched. Imagine turning it a quarter of a turn toward you, then, and you can see how the notches will fit into one another.

Figure 376. If you see that the logs are cut at, or close to, the corners (as is the case at Zakopane), you can be sure that there is a system of interlocking joinery in the interior of the joint, without which, the logs could be easily forced out of place by lateral stresses and strains.

Dovetail Joints

Figure 376a.

Dovetail Joints

The most difficult aspect of dovetail joinery is not in the cutting of the joints, but rather, in their accurate tracing. So, to simplify the tracing, I have opted for a technique drawn from my practice as a stonecutter—the use of a "template." Without this, it is of course possible (and was probably a common practice) to find the principal points by measuring and to subsequently join these points with pencil traits; but the use of a template guarantees that you will always have the same-shaped joint from one log to another, and this diminishes the risk of error. You will then always have a constant angle at which your interlocking pieces will fit together. You still have to measure and mark your principle points, but your measurements can be quickly checked against the template, which also helps you to visualize a procedure in which it is easy to get lost otherwise.

The template can be made of any material rigid enough to maintain its form: in this case, it is from a sheet of Bristol board.

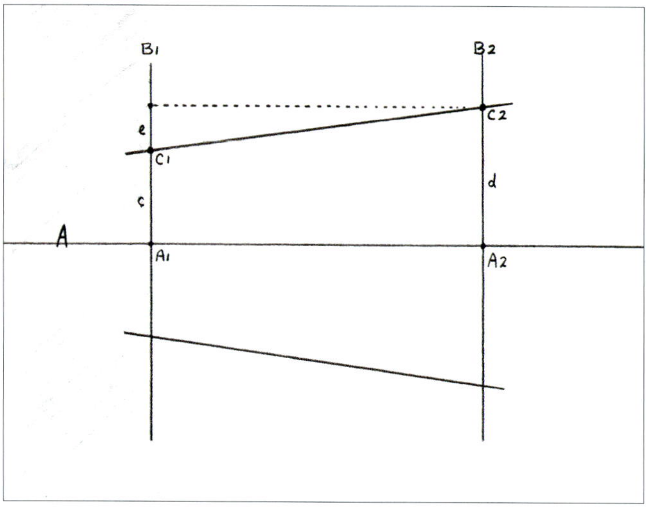

Figure 377. 1) On the Bristol board (or whatever material you choose), draw a line A which will be your horizontal axis. Then, mark out on this line point A1 and A2 so that the distance between A1 and A2 is the same as the width of the squared logs you intend to use for your wall.
For this demonstration, I am using 15 cm thick logs, and so my template measures 15 cm from A1 to A2.
2) Draw the vertical lines B1 and B2 through points A1 and A2 to make your template. These lines correspond to the inside and outside edges of your logs. The surface to the left of B1 is simply something to hold the template by while manipulating it.
3) Points C1 and C2, as well as their symmetrical counterparts on the other side of axis A, are chosen to determine the size and the angle of the dovetail. They can be placed anywhere you wish within the limits which the volume of your logs allows. The steeper the slopes of your dovetails are, the better the joints will resist sideways movement, but at the same time, "d" becomes longer, and the height of your logs will limit this dimension. I have consequently chosen the profile you see here to suit the dimensions of the logs I was using, 15 to 18 cm in height. But if you consistently use higher logs, then you can give your dovetails a more pronounced slope.
The dimensions used here, chosen to be simple to use while giving a suitable form within the limits of my logs' volumes are: C = 4 cm; d = 6 cm; and consequently, e = 2 cm.

Figure 378. The template is placed against the squared log with its horizontal axis A superimposed on the log's horizontal axis, as in the photo. To facilitate this alignment, I have cut two holes in the template to be able to see the log's axis underneath. I have also drawn other horizontal lines on either side of the original axis; any of these could serve as an alternative axis should the need arise to make a taller or a shorter dovetail without changing the angles of its faces. (I will return to this case in the demonstration).
You can now draw the outline of the dovetail by following that of the template.

Drawing the Notches

For each dovetail, you must trace three sets of lines (in any order): one on the end of the log, and one on each of its two sides.

Figure 379. ON THE SIDES
The dovetail drawn on the sides of the log always flares toward the log's end.

Figure 380. ON THE END
The dovetail drawn on the log's end always flares toward the inside of the building. Consequently, the outside of the dovetail is always thinner than the inside.

Figure 381. At the inside corner, your lines meet.

Figure 382. But on the outside corner, since the dovetail becomes thinner, your lines will not meet. You must, then, re-draw the sloping lines of the outside to compensate for this change of thickness.

Figure 383. Draw two new lines, then, on the outside of the log; they must be parallel to the others. The distance between the original lines and the redrawn lines will be the same as the dimension "e" of the template (in this case, 2 cm).
Two alternative but similar methods:

1) you can make a second template, with the slopes of the dovetail parallel to the first, but 2 cm closer to the axis. You would then use this template every time you mark the outside of the log, or:

2) using your first original template, use the alternative horizontal axes at 2 cm above and below the original axis.

Any of these methods should give the same result.

Marking Off the Notches of One Log in Relation to the Adjoining Logs

Figure 383a.

The preceding indications hold true if all of your logs have the same height. But, since in pre-industrial construction this was never the case, as the logs were squared to get the maximum height out of each, the depth to which the notches are cut must also vary so that each log will adjust optimally to its partners. The logs must thus be adjusted by perpendicular pairs, each one first with the one below, and then, once this joinery has been done, with the one above. But also, each log must descend just enough to touch the parallel log beneath it, and the distance it will descend may be different with each log.

Figure 384. To determine this: place the next log to be fitted on top of the perpendicular pair of logs it will be assembled with. Measure the distance that separates it from the parallel log beneath it, which it will end up touching. Let us call this distance "X". This same distance "X" must then be taken off out the corner joints, so that the log will descend just enough to touch the log below.

Figures 385-387. If you have already placed several logs in your wall, you may already, in the preceding log fitting, have marked out (but preferably, have not yet cut) the top part of the dovetail. (The bottom part will already have been cut and joined.)

Starting from the traits marked out, measure upward "X" at each angle of the dovetail, and mark these points on the angles of the log above.

Figures 388-389. You could equally well measure with a compass as with a ruler.

Figure 390. You can then join these points with pencil traits, and check the result against your template (placed horizontally, of course, but perhaps using one of the alternative horizontal axes to compensate for differing heights).

Figure 391. As a result, you will have the outlines of your dovetails to be fitted together, with each of their lines parallel to, and distant by "X," from its partners.

Before cutting, just be sure that your dovetails are not so thin (especially on the outside), as to be fragile. This may occur when you pass from a big log to a much smaller upper log, so it is the best to avoid important changes in log height, as you choose your logs while building. If in doubt, you can probably overcome most problems by redrawing your lines, and, instead of dividing "X" equally between the two logs, by taking more out of the bigger log and less out of the smaller, so as not to weaken it.

Figure 392. The joinery of the logs shown in the preceding page, after cutting the notches as they were marked.

Cutting the Notches

Figures 393-394. This demonstration is done on the second log from the bottom, but the method is the same for any of the logs.

It is the easiest to do the vertical cuts with a handsaw. (They can be done with a hatchet or chisel, but this takes much more time and effort.) Be careful to follow your traits precisely. As you approach the bottom of your cut, check often to be sure you are going down far enough, but not too far. Remember that your cut is on an incline, and that consequently, your saw blade will be similarly inclined when you arrive at the bottom of the cut.

Figures 395-403. Next, take out the volume of the notch as marked, using a chisel and/or an axe. Unless you are used to doing fine work with an axe, you will probably find the chisel easier to work with for cutting along the line traced on the end of the log. But once this has been done, the axe is probably a more effective tool for cutting away to your finished surface, and even for hewing to the lines on the log's side.

Figure 404. But whatever tool you choose for this work, the job will be easier if you first make one cut (or more) through the middle of the volume to be removed.

Figures 405-406. Your nearly finished surface can best be perfectly leveled with the axe head held in both hands and pushed to plane the surface. It should then be checked with a ruler (or any straight edge) to be sure that it is flat.

Other Kinds of Corner Joints

The joinery techniques above are both the most often used, and the easiest to execute for builders with limited carpentry experience. But for those who wish to seek further, other possibilities exist. In addition to those containing interlocking parts in the inside of the joints, (see pp 179 and 201-202), the photos on this page show different possibilities, and this sample is far from being a complete catalogue.

Figure 406. Peasant house from the region of Lvov, Ukraine; now in the Lvov Ethnographic Park.

Figures 407-408. Church from the Maramureş province of Romania.

Figure 409. Church from the Maramures region of Romania.

Mortise and Tenon

Figure 410

Figures 411a-411b. On the principal beam, that to which another is to be joined, mark off a rectangle which will be hollowed out to make the mortise.

In the case illustrated here, we have positioned it in the beams central axis, but this is not obligatory if other factors make a different placing preferable (for instance, if a third beam also joins the others at this point). Just be sure that the hollow you are about to make is not so close to an edge of the beam that a weak spot results. The large dimension of the rectangle will be the same as that of the piece to be inserted, or, to make a neater-looking joint, a bit less (about 6 to 12 mm at each end).

In this case, the tenon will also be reduced to fit the hole, and when it is inserted, the hole of the mortise will not be visible.

Figure 1

Figure 2

Figure 3

Figure 4

Figure 5

Figure 6

Figures 412-417. The tenon will be thinner than the beam from which it is cut, and so its outline should be traced on three of the beam's surfaces (above, below, and on the end).

As it is usual for all similar cutting operations, the cuts made across the fibers are most easily done with the handsaw (1). To cut away the rest, you may also use the saw in the direction parallel to the fibers, or take it off with a chisel (2, 3, 4), but in either case, be very careful if the fibers run into the zone you wish to leave intact.

As was indicated above, the joint will be neater looking if the tenon is reduced a bit, both in its height and in its breadth, from the dimensions of the beam from which it is cut. The mortise is measured out to correspond to this (with an additional 0.5 to 1 mm of play) and will thus be invisible once the tenon is inserted (5) and (6).

Figure 1

Figure 2

Figure 3

Figure 4

Figure 5

Cutting Out the Mortise

Specialized mortising tools exist, and were part of the carpenter's equipment in former times, but are not easily found in hardware stores today. Nonetheless, all of this work can be done quite well with a chisel. Some carpenters prefer to drill series of holes, as big and as close to one another as possible, to remove a maximum amount of wood, even before beginning work with the chisel.

Figures 418-422. Start by marking off the outline of the mortise with blows to the chisel, placed with its cutting edge along the pencil lines, the angled side to the inside of the mortise. (1) (The flat side, consequently, will descend straight down to form the inside surface of the mortise).

Once you have defined and cut down a bit (at least 5 mm.) along the outlines of the mortise, (1), you can then start cutting out wood by working inside this outline in a direction parallel to the length of the beam (2). You should alternate sequences of taking off the wood like this and cutting straight down along the inside walls of the mortise (3, 4) to go progressively deeper. The shallower the angle of the chisel, the easier it is to bite off pieces of wood, but the restrained space in which you can place your chisel will limit its movements. Change directions from time to time to better dig out, and approach each end wall from the opposite side of the mortise. You can cut as deeply as you want, as long as you make sure you do not cut through the beam, or into the space of another mortise. A light chamfer around the end of the tenon (which can be done by simply passing over the edges with a rasp) makes it easier to fit it in.

Dowels

The diameter of a dowel will be chosen in keeping with the dimensions of the beams in which the mortise and tenon are cut: I am used to seeing about 20 mm for most work with medium size beams. The dowel is a small piece of hard wood, often oak, cut roughly to a cylindrical form tapering slightly at one end for easier penetration. The holes through which they pass and jam into place must be drilled far enough from all edges of the mortise and from the end of the tenon that these do not break off or split when the dowel is driven in. The fit must be tight, except for the tapered end, which will pass through the entire assembly. The protruding ends may be cut off, if the carpenter wishes, once the final assembly has been done.

Figures 423-425. The hole is first drilled through the mortise, and then the tenon inserted, cut short enough that it does not butt against the inside end of the mortise, and will enable the two beams to fit tight at their junction point. With a long pencil, or with chalk or charcoal dust, the carpenter marks precisely the position of the hole on the tenon. It is then withdrawn, and the hole is made slightly offset (by 1 or 2 mm) from the mark, so that when the dowel is driven in, it will draw the beam bearing the tenon tightly against the beam receiving it. The fit can be verified by putting the dowel in place, without forcing it.

Figure 426. This full-scale model of carpenters assembling a wall on a tracing floor is displayed at the Alsatian Ecomuseum, France.

Assembling the Elements

The entire portion of wall or rafter structure must be assembled together before any dowels are driven in tightly: this requires a certain play between the pieces, and so the dowels, once their correct fit has been verified, will be removed during the adjusting process. This is usually done on a floor on which the assembly plan has been drawn full scale. The carpenters can then see which pieces must be assembled and in what order, because this is not arbitrary. (See the following example.) Once all the problems have been resolved, the dowels can be forced tightly into place, and the protruding ends cut off (this is optional). If ever one has to be removed, it can be knocked out with mallet blows on the tapering end. If this has been cut, then another dowel can be used to chase it. In fact, post and beam constructions were sometimes entirely disassembled to be remounted at a different site according to the changing needs of the owners.

Assembling Braces with Mortise and Tenon Joinery

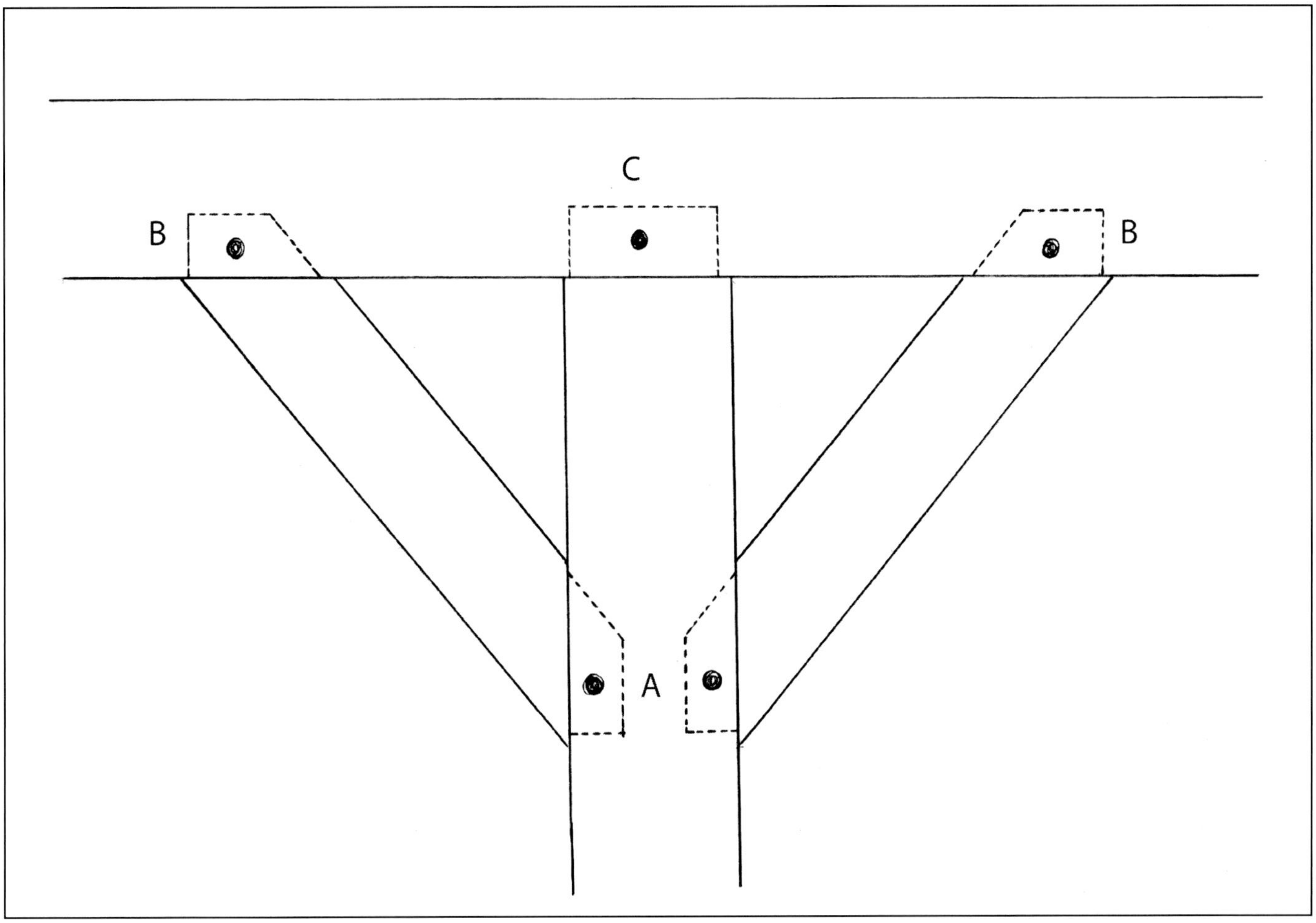

Figure 427.

A: The tenons are cut horizontally at their lower ends (A) to be able to slide horizontally into the mortises of the post. The post must not be weakened by making the mortises too deep.

B: The tenons are cut vertically at B, to be able to slide vertically into the upper sill.

C: Fitting order:

1) The braces are first slid horizontally into the post at A.
2) Next, the upper sill slides down onto the other pieces, which fit into it at B. This is usually done with all the pieces laid flat on a tracing floor with the dowels removed so that there is some play between the pieces.
3) Then, the dowels are driven into place to consolidate the structure.

Figure 428. *Savoy, France*

Preparing the Wood

Trees were traditionally cut in winter — some say as the moon was waning, others say at the new moon — in any case, at a time of maximum contraction of the tree and its sap.

Pine trees for building came preferably from areas unfavorable for growth (in Russia, from sandy soils; in Norway, from zones of high altitude). In such conditions, the trees grow relatively slowly and their annual growth rings are consequently closer together than those of fast-growing trees, resulting in a denser, more resistant wood.

As for those regions where oak is predominant, the forests used as timber suppliers (principally for shipbuilding, secondarily for houses) were managed in a way that the growth was very dense, and often interspersed with beech trees. The result of this forestry practice was to force the trees to grow straight and tall toward the light of the sky.

It is the best to build with wood as dry as possible; this minimizes the problems of shrinkage and warping, allows tight-fitting joinery that will not contract, and also makes handling easier, as dry logs are much lighter. On the other hand, the wood becomes harder upon drying (in the case of oak, very hard indeed), so the logs were usually squared while still green. They could then be stockpiled and separated by shims to allow air to circulate on all sides of each log. The weight created by piling also helps minimize warping, if the logs have been squared; any squared logs at the top of a pile will probably twist as they dry. The (natural) drying process has to be very slow. The summer sun has to be avoided, and even so, the logs should be wet down often to control the drying process during hot periods.

Most of the drying takes place in the first two years after felling, although the process continues, to a lesser extent, for five years. It was common, then, for a peasant who already had a place to live to set aside a stock of building wood to dry for two years or more. But for the pioneer, whether he be eighteenth or nineteenth century American moving westward, medieval French forest-clearer, or German colonist of the fourteenth century moving eastward, this was rarely possible. They would try to arrive in their chosen region as early as possible in the springtime, quickly construct a shelter, sow crops in a field prepared by felling trees, and then use these trees to construct a house that would be habitable for the coming winter. This house, made necessarily of green (undried) wood, would be imperfectly assembled after the wood had dried, shrunk, and possibly warped. The house would probably also be too small for a comfortable permanent dwelling, and would often be relegated to use as a storage shed or a stable when the family had resolved the more pressing problems of survival and could take the time to construct a proper house.

The bark should be removed soon after felling; this makes the drying easier, but especially, avoids giving a comfortable abode to insects, who like to lodge in the cavity between the bark and the wood when this begins to shrink.

The bark can be removed in one of several ways:

1) With an axe: used gently with skill, the axe can be used to lift off the bark without cutting into the tree trunk.
2) With a drawknife.
3) With a bark-peeling spade, a tool with a long handle on which is mounted a square metal plate (like a spade). This tool enables one to work without bending over. The spade is slipped underneath the bark, and peels it off while sliding over the harder wood of the trunk beneath.

The Problems of Wood Shrinkage

While a log will shrink by about 2.5% through its diameter, it scarcely retracts at all through its length. A log wall, consequently, will reduce in height by about 5 cm for a 2 meter wall over a period of several years; but the vertical elements such as door and window jambs will not follow this movement. The builder must consequently allow the horizontal logs to slide within grooves in the vertically placed elements; he must also leave a space (which at first will be filled with a compressible insulating material) to permit the logs above these elements to settle downwards and not touch the vertical pieces until the drying process is complete. Until then, these logs will descend 1 to 2 cm each year, and they must not find themselves blocked on top of a doorjamb while the logs below continue to descend, opening up a gap. (While this gap, it is true, could be filled with the insulating material, this would be a permanent condition, whereas the space left above the doorjambs is only temporary.)

Another potential problem occurs at the corners where the logs protrude beyond the point at which they join. Those parts of the logs which remain outside of the building do not receive the warmth produced within, and will dry less quickly, shrinking less. Those parts of the logs receiving the inside warmth will consequently shrink more, and gaps can open up between them. It is best, then, to leave about 1 cm (0.5 inch) of space between these protruding ends by trimming off that much more when making the groove underneath during the construction process (see *"The Round Notch"* in *The Carpenter's Handbook*). These gaps on the outside will have no incidence on the thermal efficiency of the building, and will reduce to nothing after a few years.

Using Mechanized Tools

Those wishing to build with squared logs but not wanting to execute the long and physically trying work of dressing them with an axe can buy machine-sawn lumber from a sawmill or building supplies yard. The lumber can also be "milled," that is, planed mechanically; in this way, much time is saved, as well as wear on the back. The machine-cut lumber will be smooth and regular in appearance, which some builders may appreciate and others deplore. Manual work, on the other hand, necessitates working each piece, taking into account its particularities. The round logs are never perfect cylinders, all looking the same. The squared logs each have different heights, and often, irregularly rounded angles. The elements of a post and beam half-timbered framework are not always straight. Pre-industrial buildings, then, by their very lack of uniformity, do not look like factory-made products. If you like the buildings you see illustrated in this book, then, you should be wary of the uniformity of milled lumber.

Commonly Used Modern Machine Tools

The chain saw seems to be an indispensable tool for professional builders wanting to increase their earnings as well as for any amateur builder wishing to spend the minimum amount of time necessary to get the job done. It can be used to speed up the work at several stages, including:

— Cutting logs.
— Making all the vertical saw cuts for cutting out notches as shown in the chapter *"The Carpenter's Handbook."* Sometimes this mass has to be removed with a chisel after the preliminary cuts have been made, but in some cases, the mass can also be cut out with the chain saw manipulated obliquely and the bottoms, round or flat, finished by running the chain saw over them in a sideways back-and-forth movement, scraping the surfaces (in the case of a simple joint with no internal, interlocking notches).
— Scoring a log for squaring or for dressing a side. This will be done with simple saw cuts instead of the V-cuts done with an axe. In fact, the entire squaring process can be done with a chain saw, but unless you wish to at least finish the visible surfaces with hand tools, you may as well have the logs squared by the sawmill with its powerful and accurate circular saws.

In considering the time saved by working with a chain saw, however, you should take into account the time necessary for frequently sharpening the chain (each individual tooth requiring filing). Other disadvantages are: the noise (often more disturbing for other people sharing your space than for yourself) and keeping supplied with oil and gasoline, which must be stored and frequently manipulated.

Afterword

Some Thoughts about Manual Work

The road (unpaved until recently) ends 300 meters before my house; a dirt track leads the rest of the way. On one side is a state forest, on another, a cliff. The electric line was never brought to this house, the last before a no-building zone and 500 meters beyond the preceding one. When I first moved in, my finances would not allow me to pay for the extension of the line, and in any case, I didn't care much about it. Now that I can afford it, I still don't feel the need for it. I had already made the choice, which moving into that house twenty-five years ago only confirmed: I want to work natural materials with hand tools. This choice was made for pleasure rather than out of ideological purism: I do buy stones cut mechanically at the quarry because I find quarry-work hard and unrewarding, and personally, I do not wish to do it. On the other hand, I felt inspired by the medieval stonecutter's and carpenter's callings. And while it seems to me desirable to be frugal with industrial energy in view of our century's social, economic, and ecological problems, I rarely sacrificed my desires through idealism; I simply wanted to do satisfying work in the most pleasant conditions possible. To me, this meant avoiding what I often saw in stonecutters' workshops: machine noise, dust in the air and powder over everything, unsightly aluminum sheds and machines cluttering up the environment, and on top of it all, important debts for all the mechanical equipment (which no bank would have granted me, moreover). To preserve my environment in the way I like it, I am willing to work a bit longer to accomplish the same quantity of work, especially since I find the work more pleasant under these conditions. The choice of manual work is thus more of an affective choice, often contradictory to the logic of productivity. But for me, I like to feel my link with the builders of ancient times, and with a tradition of over a thousand years.

My wish for this book is that it gives you pleasure to contemplate the beauty of these products of an earlier age, and enables you to better appreciate the skills that went into their realization. And for those who also see themselves as inheritors of this thousand-year tradition, I hope it will help your own projects take form. I would be glad to know that it has inspired others to build houses or other buildings that give them a sense of satisfaction, while also making their (and our collective) environment more beautiful.

To further this, I have created a website where I can give you any new information I learn, reply to your questions (or leave these open for replies from other readers), and enable you to share your experiences, discoveries, and accomplishments. The address is: www.architrad-books.com

Wishing you happy trails,
David Campbell, Aix-en- Provence,
May 1, 2007

Figure 429. ***Stara Lubovna Ethnographic Park (Skanzen), Slovakia.***

Ethnomuseums

(Ecomuseums, Open Air Museums, Ethnographic Parks)

In many countries, starting with Sweden and then Norway toward the end of the nineteenth century, teams of ethnologists, doubting the survival of their traditional arts and crafts in a rapidly evolving world, began to collect interesting old buildings destined for demolition and to reassemble them in other sites where they would be part of open air museums. In these museums ("open air" because the structures on exhibit were much too big to be contained under a roof), an effort was made not only to restore the buildings, but also to present them in an environment similar to that of their original sites, often with farm buildings disposed around a main dwelling according to the local traditions. The grounds are often quite vast – over 60 or even 100 acres. In many, museum employees can be seen performing peasant chores or handicrafts, and the grass is cut and the meadows maintained with a scythe. The houses are usually furnished in accordance with their time period, and are often open for a look inside. There is no mud, nor (rarely) any piles of manure, which makes walking around these parks quite pleasant, although giving a somewhat romanticized view of peasant life.

Most countries of Eastern Europe and Scandinavia have a national museum close to the capital (Oslo, Copenhagen, Stockholm, Helsinki, Tallinn, Riga, Kiev, and Bucharest), where houses (or sometimes entire farmsteads) representative of the country's different regional particularities can be seen. And, in various places throughout the country, regional museums may also be found. The following list gives the addresses of those I know. There are undoubtedly others of which I don't know; if they (or you) write me, I will post them on my web site (www.architrad-books.com). Their web sites are also furnished, where I was able to find them. Some do not have an official site, but you can get some information about them through travel agency sites, from *Wikipedia*, or from *virtualtourist* by searching for "open air museum" and adding the name of the place concerned.

Some of those listed are not really museums, but rather centers of applied research, specialized in a theme or in a time period; this will then be noted.

List of Ethnomuseums

CZECH REPUBLIC

Rožnov pod Radhoštem
Wallachian ethnological museum
www.vmp.cz/english/default.htm
(regional)

DENMARK

Aarhus
Den Gamle By (The Old Town)
Viborgvej 2
www.dengamleby.dk
(museum of urban architecture)

Albertslund (about 25 km west of Copenhagen)
Vikingelandsbyen
www.vikingelandsbyen.dk
(research and pedagogic centre specializing in Viking history and culture)

Copenhagen (Lyngby)
Frilandsmuseet (The Open Air Museum)
Kongevejen 100
www.natmus.dk
(national ethnographic museum of Denmark)

Lejre (about 50 km west of Copenhagen)
Lejre Archeological Research Center)
Slangeallee 2
www.lejre-center.dk
(research and pedagogic centre specializing in the Bronze and Iron Ages)

ESTONIA

Tallinn (Rocca al Mare)
Estonian National Ethnographic Museum
Vabaohumuusemi tee 12
www.evm.ee

FRANCE

Beynac (Dordogne)
Beynac Archeological Park
Chemin du Chateau
http://perso.orange.fr/parc.beynac/parc.beynac.htm
(research and pedagogic center specializing in the Bronze and Iron Ages)

Crèvecoeur-en-Auge (Calvados)
Chateau de Crèvecoeur
www.chateau-de-crevecoeur.com
(museum and pedagogic center specializing in regional culture and architecture)

Ungersheim (Haut Rhin)
Ecomusée d'Alsace (Alsatian Ethnographic Museum)
Chemin du Grosswald
www.ecomusee-alsace.fr
(regional ethnographic park)

FINLAND

Helsinki (Seurasaari)
Seurasaari Open Air Museum
www.nba.fi/en/seurasaari_openairmuseum
(national ethnographic museum of Finland)

LATVIA

Riga
Brivdabas Museum
440 Brivibas Gatve
www.virmus.lv
www.itg.lv/english/brivdabas.musejs
(national ethnographic museum of Latvia)

NORWAY

Eidsborg (Telemark; near Dalen)
West Telemark Museum
www.vest-telemark.museum.no
(regional ethnographic park)

Fagernes (Valdres)
Valdres museum
Tyinvegen 27

Lillehammer (Gudbrandsdalen)
Maihaugen Museum
Maihaugeveien 1
www.maihaugen.no
(regional ethnographic park)

Nesbyen (Hallingdal)
Hallingdal Museum
www.hallingdal-museum.no
(regional ethnographic park)

Oslo (Bygdøy)
Norske Folkemuseum
Museumsveien 10, Bygdøy
(national ethnographic museum of Norway)

POLAND

Novy Sacz

(regional ethnographic park)

Sanok

Sanok Ethnographic Park

(regional)

Zakopane

Tatra Museum

www.muzeumtatrzanskie.com.pl

(regional ethnographic museum with several sites, including the Jurgow Meadows)

ROMANIA

Baia Mare (Maramureş)

Baia Mare Museum of Ethnography and Folk Arts

http://www.maramuresmuzeu.ro/ro/index.php

(regional)

Cluj-Napoca

Transylvania Ethnographic museum, ethnographic park Romulus Vuia

www.muzeul-etnografic.ro

(regional)

Sibiu (Dumbrava, à 8 km distant)

Ethnographic Museum Astra

www.muzeulastra.ro

(regional)

Sighetul Marmatiei

Maramureş Museum (Open Air section, about 4 km from town)

(regional)

RUSSIA

Kizhi (Carelia)

Kizhi State Museum of Wooden Architecture

http://kizhi.karelia.ru

(regional)

(Velikaya) Novgorod

Vitoslavlitsy Ethnographic Park

(regional)

SLOVAKIA

Bardejov

Šariš Museum, Bardejov (Open Air Section at Bardejovske Kupele, about 5 km from town)

www.muzeumbardejov.sk

(regional)

Stara Lubovna

Lubovna Museum (*Skanzen*, the open air section)

www.muzeumsl.sk

(regional)

Svidnik

Museum of Ukranian Culture

www.muk.sk

(regional museum dedicated to the Ruthenian ethnic group)

SWEDEN

Hollviken (about 20 km south of Malmö)

Foteviken Museum and Viking Reserve

www.foteviken.se

(reconstitution of life during Viking times)

Lund (about 25 km northeast of Malmö)

Kulturen (Museum of Cultural History)

www.kulturen.com

(regional)

Stockholm (Djurgården)

Skansen

www.skansen.se

(national ethnographic park)

SWITZERLAND

Brienz (about 50 km southeast of Bern)

Ballenberg Museum

www.ballenberg.ch

(national ethnographic park)

UKRAINIA

Kiev (Pirogovo)

Museum of Ukrainian Folk Life and Architecture

(national)

L'vov

L'vov Museum of Folk Life and Architecture

(regional)

Chernechka Gora 1

Shevchevensky Hai

Pereieslav-Khmilnietski (about 6à km south of Kiev)

Pereieslav-Khmilnietski Museum of Folk Life and Architecture

(regional)

The photo p. 111 was taken at Black Creek Pioneer Village,
Mississauga (Toronto), Ontario, Canada
www.blackcreek.ca
(regional open air museum of eighteenth and nineteenth century life)

Acknowledgments

My thanks to:

Juan Ocampo Rosales: Stonecutter in Taxco, Mexico, who welcomed me as a guest at his home in 1977, and taught me the basis of stonecutting and sculpture;

Stephane De Asis: Stonecutter in Haute Provence—who was my associate during my formative years;

Professors George Bunker (the owner) and Louis Frey (my neighbour): both now deceased, who allowed me to live and work at the Maison du Rocher in the Bibemus stone quarry from 1980 onward, and to the City of Aix-en-Provence, who, after receiving the property as a legacy, allowed me to continue my work and residency there;

Annie Peltriaux: For having taught me to use a computer, and for her moral support;

All the ethnographic museums visited for existing, and notably to the architect Arek Kryda of Sanok and guides Natalia, Dimitri, and Rita at Kizhi, Natasha at Kiev (Pirogovo), jancu remus at Sibiu, and Laurent Bernat at Beynac for their help;

Bo Jørgen Nielsen and Øystein Kosveit: For taking me to visit several interesting sites in Denmark and Norway, respectively;

Architect Jan Karpiel Bułecka: For allowing me to visit an interesting building site in Zakopane;

Sacha Krasilnikov: of Sortavala: For having integrated me in his carpentry crew at Kizhi Island during several weeks;

Father Nikolai Ozolin: For his hospitality during one of my stays in Kizhi;

and carpenters Piotr Popiel at Sanok, and Sacha, Nikolai, and Liousha, at Kizhi: For having allowed me to observe and photograph their work.